Puck You!

Puck You!

Walking the Crooked Path of Queer Resistance

Sven Davisson

Rebel Satori Press

SATOR pentagram on page 194 from Pseudo-Solomon, mid-18th century, ms. 4666 in the Wellcome Collection.

Cover & book design by Sven Davisson

Paperback ISBN: 978-1-60864-357-8

Published in the United States of America by
Arabi Manor
A Rebel Satori Imprint
www.rebelsatoripress.com

This book is dedicated to my beloved
Nathaniel Davisson, to all my brothers
in the New Orleans's Grove, and to the
ancestors upon whose shoulders we stand.

Contents

Foreword
Invocation
Meditation

Resistance   1
Ancient Custom   11
The Crooked Path   15
The Holy Covenant   27
The Sabbath   33
The Red Meal   39
The Elder Gods   47
The (K)Ing of the Ælfe   59
Spirits of Place   73
Outside the Fence   79
Immolation & Emanation   83
The Guardian   89
The Revenants   95
The Black Dog   105
The Smithy   119
The Ward Cubes   125
Squaring the Compass   129
Hallowing the Blade   137

The Hazel Wand 145

Sitting Out 153

Activating the Stave 161

Violet Elixir 167

Skimmed Water Ointment 173

The Threshold 177

Befriending the Fae 183

Oberon's Plate 187

The Devil's Square 195

Interlude 199

The Field Remedy 207

In the Dark 215

The Repast 221

The Dumb Supper 227

Foreword

hroughout history, witch-
craft has been an act of
resistance. It has been the
whispered spell in the dark,
the quiet defiance of those
who refuse to be powerless,
the sacred knowledge passed down despite
oppression. To practice magic is to claim
agency over oneself and one's world—to
push back against forces that seek to
control, suppress, or diminish.

This book is a guide for those who
walk the path of the witch not only as
a seeker of wisdom and power but as a
force for change. Magical resistance is an
act of survival, a form of rebellion, and a
declaration of sovereignty over one's own
spirit. Whether through spellwork, ritual,
sigils, or the simple act of standing firm

in your truth, magic offers tools to shape reality in alignment with justice, freedom, and personal empowerment.

In these pages, you will find wisdom and defiance drawn from the enduring legacy of witches who came before us. This is not just a book—it is a call to action, an invocation of power, and a reminder that magic is, at its core, transformative.

May you find strength in these words, courage in your practice, and the unshakable knowing that your magic—your resistance—matters.

Dave Gaddy
March, 2025

Lord, what fools these mortals be!

– Puck

Invocation

The Wild Boys and Port of Saints formed my initiation into the land of plague and the bardo. I find myself at these sometimes treacherous crossroads on the path toward immortality. My visions, tinged with whisky, reveal new myths, scars, and magic. I chant your words like a mantra. The sound of rain blankets my thoughts: I hear its steady drip from the eaves onto the condensers. The warm glow of candles is accompanied by the faint suburban light from outside. The scents of pomegranate and cassis, Parfum d'Or, linger in the air. La Madama. Fortuna. Lady Luck. Memories scurry through the walls like rats, reminding me of all the nights spent typing, cutting, and pasting zines. Now, in the candlelight, I lay down the Nine of Cups. I light a blue candle to open the road—blue, a color symbolizing the intersection of memory and prosperity in the octarine spectrum of magic.

Mektoub— it is written.

Meditation

e may feel miserable because we get too wrapped up in our sense of self. So, what does it mean? When we become consumed by our individuated identities, we create a divide between ourselves and the world around us. We become like islands when we draw invisible lines between what we perceive as "me" and what is "not me."

This self-centric view isolates us and blocks our natural flow. It's as if we've become frozen, lacking the warmth and connection that bring life to our experience. Love and joy are the essence of what makes us human, yet when we're rigid in ourselves, we often distance ourselves from these feelings. We may fear that if we allow love in and embrace joy, our carefully constructed boundaries will begin to fade. At first, this can be unsettling. Distance and closing off can provide a false sense of safety.

But there's a beautiful truth: it's through love, joy, and their extension in kindness that we truly experience our innate freedom. When we open ourselves up to these feelings, the walls we've built around ourselves begin to melt away. Instead of being like ice, we can be vibrant and flowing. The path from cold isolation embraces warmth and connection with others. As we risk opening ourselves, we move beyond the limitations of an isolated sense of self and step onto a path that opens to a world filled with love, growth, and possibility.

Our lives are filled with ups and downs, darkness and light.

Observe the ocean waves. The higher they rise, the more profound the low that follows. One moment, you are soaring at the crest, and the next, you find yourself in the serene hollowness of the trough. Embrace both experiences; don't become fixated on one. Avoid thinking, "I want to stay in this high forever." That's a fantasy. It's simply not how life works. It's a truth: peaks are fleeting, and so are valleys. When the peaks come, savor their beauty, but when you slip into the valleys, appreciate that too. There's nothing wrong with the low points. Valleys can be moments that allow time for reflection. Peaks are exhilarating, but living in constant excitement isn't sustainable. So, relish every moment—whether you're on top of the world or finding peace in the depths below. Each has its beauty and purpose.

There is a path through the wasteland. It's a crooked path—bent and queer. Connecting with our past lives, ancestors, and craft brothers, we build relationships that lift us out of ourselves and the occluding maelstrom that sometimes seems to swirl around us. The vagaries of time are like breezes that blow against us as we walk along. Sometimes, they may feel like profound headwinds, but they are blustery and refreshing in others.

Resistance

e have always been the crone living at the edge of the village or the cave in the woods. Our natural realms are at the fringe. No matter how much our hopes are dashed, we must remind ourselves that this liminal domain is our space and from whence we draw much of our power. We are the hare in the verge and the rider of the hedge. Our innate stance is resistance.

The war against witches is often mischaracterized as a war on women. This simplification occludes and obscures the historical fact that eradication of supernatural evil frequently targeted gender transgression and sexual deviance. It was a conflict that focused on difference and turned neighbor against neighbor. The village healer could all too quickly become the evil conjurer sowing deprivation, stealing milk, and cursing livestock. The power to heal meant that the witch also had the power to harm. To deviate sexually was a conspiracy with the Devil. The sodomite became sorcerer. The infernal kiss was at the heart of the witches's sabbath.

Buggery is a pact.

The arc of progress may bend toward justice, but it's not a straight path. Progress is often contentious and fraught with danger. There have been and will continue to be aberrations along the way. Progress is a complex struggle; the ideals of justice and equity are not straightforawrd to achieve. History has born witness to numerous setbacks and deviations. The path toward justice is anything but linear. These aberrations serve as stark reminders of the fragility of progress.

The retrograde motion of progress is

all too often ugly, even horrific. But like Mercury, it only appears to move backward at times. Though society's trajectory may sometimes seem to regress, these periods can also provide crucial opportunities for reflection, reevaluation, and, ultimately, resistance. These dark times can inflict real trauma and leave scars. Yet, just as Mercury's apparent backward motion is part of a larger, cyclical journey, so too is our struggle for progress an ongoing process.

It is essential to sustain hope, recognizing that every challenge faced is a step in the collective journey toward a more just society. Each setback may reveal hidden truths and strengthen resolve, fueling the drive for change. In this way, the path to justice—while at times fraught with obstacles—remains a vital and worthwhile pursuit, marked by both struggle and triumph. Throughout history, we have witnessed numerous setbacks and deviations from the desired course—instances where the momentum of positive change has stalled or even reversed, demonstrating that the path to justice is anything but a straight line.

Many people live in fear, and the myth of safety is often sold to them in an alluring package. Violent mobs are not as big a threat as those who transform fear into obedience. History has shown that dark magic is at work. The masses may be ignorant, but it is essential to remember that ignorance is not a lack of knowledge but a particular type of knowing. It is shaped and cultivated from the outside for a purpose.

The Weimar Republic was Germany's first experiment at a liberal democratic government. Hitler attempted a violent coup in 1923. He failed and was sentenced to prison only to be democratically elected in 1936. National Socialism mobilized an unstable economy and rampant inflation coupled with the evocation of latent xenophobia and anti-semitism to deliver their victory. These aberrant deviations to progress's arc are often viewed as eruptions of barbarism, as backward movement. The contrary is all too often true.

The worst episodes of the past century were products of modernity, not throwbacks to a dark, distant past. The mass deportation of millions of people only begins with defining the other—the enemy within. Fear is a critical first step that buys the complacency of the many. But it is only that, a first step. The expulsion of that number of people is administratively and mechanistically impossible. The architects of the Final Solution were administrators and bureaucrats—paper pushers—not demons. They leveraged the advancements of the Industrial Revolution and modernity to accomplish their delegated goal. Innovation seems like progress, but technology and technological advancements are neutral in and of themselves. How they are put to use defines their relativism.

With all the efficiency of the modern bureaucratic state, the administrators of the Third Reich utilized the industrial rail system and Henry Ford's innovative assembly line. Exterminating a million individuals at the end of a rifle is impossible, but they proved it easy enough with the stroke of a pen.

Of course, the Nazis may have started with the Jews, but they did not stop there. The Night of the Long Knives, which took place from June 30 to July 2, 1934, targeted the SA (Sturmabteilung), the Nazi Party's original paramilitary wing. This series of political extrajudicial executions allowed Hitler to consolidate his power and eliminate potential threats within the Nazi Party.

One of the main targets was Ernst Röhm, the leader of the SA, who was a close ally of Hitler but was seen as a threat due to his ambitions and the SA's increasing power. Röhm's known homosexuality was used as a pretext for his execution. During the purge, many SA leaders and other perceived opponents were arrested and executed. The purge also marked the beginning of systematic persecution of homosexuals by the Nazi regime, which intensified after Röhm's death.

On May 6, 1933, Nazi-supporting youth

looted the Magnus Hirschfeld Institute for Sexual Research, founded in 1919. A few days later, the entire contents of its library were burned. This event was part of a broader campaign by the Nazis to destroy "un-German" literature, which included works on homosexuality and gender. The destruction of the institute's library resulted in the loss of invaluable research and documentation on LGBTQ+ issues.

Hirschfeld, who was both Jewish and gay, was targeted by the Nazis and forced into exile. His life's work was largely destroyed, but his contributions to the field of sexology and LGBTQ+ rights remain.

During the Nazi regime, an estimated 100,000 men were arrested for homosexuality. Of these, around 50,000 were convicted, and many were sent to concentration camps. The death toll among these prisoners is estimated to be between 5,000 and 15,000.

The tragic irony is that after World War II, the situation for homosexual men did not improve significantly. Many of those who had been imprisoned for homosexuality were not recognized as victims of Nazi persecution and were often forced to serve out their prison sentences. Reparations were generally denied, and the stigma and legal persecution continued for many years.

Many homosexuals who the Nazis had imprisoned were transferred to regular prisons after the regime fell. The persecution of homosexuals did not end with the fall of the Nazi regime. Paragraph 175, the law that criminalized homosexuality, remained in effect in West Germany until 1969.

It is important to not passively sit back and think this too shall pass. The sentiment that we have survived dark times before is less than helpful. Not all of us survived the Reagen era genocide of indifference. We lost a generation of gay men.

Even in challenge, the path remains ahead and not just behind. A dim light shows us the way forward, even in the darkest hour.

Resistance is not futile;
it is essential.

Ancient Custom

ne of my earliest teachers was my great aunt Ruth Moore, Uppy to our family. She penned a series of sapphic sonnets, which she wrote in 1936 and published in 1972, called "The Mountain of Snow." In Sonnet III, she encourages her lover to "be not ashamed nor over-proud that ancient custom cradles you to bed."

Her admonishment is honest. There should be no shame in our desire, nor should we have too much pride in our journey. As witch brothers, we do cloak ourselves in ancient customs. We may be bad-ass witches, but a little humility never hurts. It allows critical headspace for empathy.

In the same sonnet, she writes, "This is not new; it is only new to you." Our love, she writes, is "older than the primeval cloud/When the first tiger sprang, the first wound bled..." Gay identity may be a modern social construct, but our desire is older than the pyarmids and standing stones. It is elemental.

Necessity means we must weave our own stories. We forge modern myths from ancient ore.

The crooked path is an ancient road.

The primeval enfolds us. It swaths us in a dense cloak of safety. Our stories preserve and propel us. They are not mere words but survival. Each story affords us a unique perspective on the human world. They help us to see the natural as ever-present and populated by old powers. Our new mythologies give us strength and courage in modernity's darkest hours.

Even if we must pass them mouth to ear; they are ours, and no one can steal our stories. They preserve us. Our stories honor the ancient ones and imbue the present with their time-honed wisdom.

These stories weave ancient threads

into the fabric of the modern. The witch's path operates outside normal time, and our work transcends the temporal.

We are made of dust and earth-like things. Ancestral memory brings old dreams that aged before the world began.

Our practice begins with ourselves. The Buddhists have a prayer known as Metta:

May I be free of suffering;
    may I feel safe and still.
May I be free of enmity,
    loving, grateful, and kind.
May I be healthy
    and at ease in all my ills.
May I be at peace,
    embracing all conditions of life.

The prayer is repeated three times. The first is I, the second is they, and the third is we. The trifold pattern reminds us that empathy for others begins with kindness to the self. Our safety comes first. Our sanity and stability are paramount. The journey begins with our own self-care.

The Crooked Path

he Crooked Path is a safe space to be unsafe. There are times when we walk the path in solitude. We can let our guard down and reflect in these moments. There are other times when we walk this path in community with our brothers. In their company, we may also learn to seek our true selves. We can let our guard down and be ourselves. The fraternal bower is self-supporting.

As we walk on, we come to a small clearing surrounded by a border of evergreen. For, the path traverses a discursive field. Our journey empowers us to tell our stories. Some of the most poignant moments of our coven gatherings are the minutes after cakes and wine when we sit and talk

surrounded by spirit and the ancestors.

Memory is our birthright. Our history is our own.

In days not so long before our own, epic journeys were depicted on tapestries. They were the cellphone cameras of their age. As we walk, we combine the threads of past and future into our own weaving. The warp is our past, memory, and ancient custom. The weft is potential. As it passes through the shed, the space between the warp threads, it combines with the many threads of memory and custom, transforms into the present moment, and instantly becomes memory.

As we progress in our work, we realize that we craft our own tales. History, custom, and memory are but materials, unwoven wool or undyed yarn. They are ours to craft our own unique narratives. As ancient custom carries us to bed, it also gives us the agency to dream our own myths from its bones.

Fate may spin the warp threads, but from our history, we spin the weft and, through experience, can learn how to adjust the shed rods. Thus, we can change the set and alter the resulting pattern.

There will inevitably be times when we face the three of swords. Feelings of sorrow and depression traditionally mark this card. At these times, we may feel hard-pressed to find any glimmer of hope in the current situation. It is good to remind ourselves that we may be the center of our universe, but we are not the only piece on the game board.

The chess master knows how to play the long game. What is happening in the present may feel like an adverse road, but it may be just an element in a complex gambit.

It is not that we always bring dark times upon ourselves. Just as our actions do not evoke a hurricane, the dark forces coming together in seeming collusion may not be of our making. The game board has many squares, and the game can be very complex.

The tower does not collapse on its own. It is blasted by external force. The collision of energies may be entirely malignant, but the result is the same.

New creativity may arise in the iconoclastic dust of old systems and regimented hierarchies. As the walls come down, safe spaces become ever more critical. We may take refuge in our territories of queer bars and community centers. The bent road is one such haven.

Beginning around 1500 BCE, a significant transition took place among the peoples of ancient Britain. They shifted from gathering in large numbers at notable stone monuments to meeting in more intimate settings at the edges of bodies of water. This change involved making valuable offerings in streams, rivers, and ponds. During this period, the construction of causeways allowed access to sacred islands, providing ideal places for depositing these gifts.

In contrast to the feasts and celebrations that involved hundreds or even thousands of participants, evidence suggests that this new mode of worship was more personal and conducted on a smaller scale. The close grouping of offerings indicates that those making them were likely fewer in number. A priest addressing a large crowd would typically scatter offerings widely to create maximum impact. However, archaeologists have found that the placement of these new offerings was very deliberate. This suggests that worship shifted from grand spectacles to a form of reverence shared more closely among families or clans.

Bodies of water, such as streams, lakes, and ponds, have long been sacred places. Their surface is a boundary between our world and the otherworld. They are both a mirror reflecting us back to ourselves and an entrance to other realms. Going back to time before written memory, they are an entrance to the realms of the goddess. They are a doorway to the underworld of the goddess Hel.

The Lady of the Lake may be a vestigial echo of the time when swords and other prized objects were thrown into their watery depths as watery offerings. It may be that the ancestors found one of these sacrificial swords, bent and broken, and from this, the image of the spirit of the waters offering up a sword arose.

When we pause along the path and gaze upon the pond's surface, we see both a reflection of ourselves and an opportunity. If we look beyond our mirror image, we can see a portal. Our offering is reciprocated with the gift of understanding.

As we progress along our journey, we will undoubtedly encounter jealousy. From an underlying insecurity, we may face judgment from the outside. This is a natural facet of our current conditions. Weeds may just as often have thorns as produce beautiful wildflowers. The pond's edge, the meeting point of land and water, is guarded by razor-sharp sedge.

As we gain in our understanding and manifest a new empathy for others, we may feel that we carry a burden of responsibility. At times, the weight of it may feel immense. It may seem that we are asked to support not just our own but the burdens of the many. This can all too quickly overwhelm. As we ascend a rise in the path, we may have a strong sense that we carry the weight of those who have gone before, our ancestors, and those who may be following behind in our footsteps.

A residual insecurity all too often underscores this sense of burden on the surface. The conditioning of our upbringing, our interactions with schoolyard bullies, religious intolerance, threats of brimstone, and damnation may make us question our footing.

In these moments, recall that we enter the path from a point of balance. We wouldn't have found the starting point if this were not the case. The way only opens before us when the unfolding knows we are ready to begin.

We tend to cling to trauma. We instinctively fear the unknown, and all too often, we prefer the familiar, even if it is painful. The way ahead is guarded. We will meet the skeletal beast of our past. Confronting and releasing our past hurt, collective and personal, is the price of our passage.

We are the wandering fool. Our journey is not just about a leap of faith but is also one of letting go. We can not progress far carrying the summation of such weight. With each step, we leave our insecurity behind even as it attempts to nip at our heels. The fool traditionally signifies the wanderer, not because he is foolish but because he has let go of past conditioning. His eyes are open in childlike wonder at the as-yet-undefined opportunity before him. When he jumps off the cliff into the unknown, he lands on a rainbow bridge arcing over the clouds of others' ignorance.

The otter guides us in the boundary space between land and watery depths. As we progress, others may see us as the cunning fox, the sly knight of the wood.

The path is not always straight. By definition, it is crooked. Along the way, we may experience what feels like inertia and boredom. The element of magick is the animating spark that transforms inertia into motion.

Our ecstasy lifts us. We dance in the sacred compass formed of elemental forces in the company of our brothers, ancestors, and spirits.

I am the Holy Covenant.
I am the promise of flesh foretold
Thrusting forth from the formless.
I am the primal surge
In the unnamed depths.
I am the potent spark,
Dripping from the Void.
I possess the stranger
At the urinal.
We turn, kneel, and drain him.
Our mouth is his offering bowl;
Even the most earthly effluent
Holds the seed of your liberation.
I am the nothingness
That cradles the stars.
I am the black
Behind the snowflake—
Unique and unknowable,
Even as it melts.

The Holy Covenant

 covenant is an agreement, a promise. The Holy Covenant is a pact between men and their gods. A covenant is also a promise against. A critical aspect of the pact is keeping evil at bay. The Holy Covenant is a bulwark against dark forces and the rise of despotism.

The Dark Lord is the ultimate outsider. He is the Lord of Kaos, and his breath is the dry, hot wind of the south. He is also the instigator, the motivating force—the novel action of the uncanny.

When he coupled with his brother, wisdom was born.

His lustful chthonic energies balance the lawful, ordered forces of rigid hierarchical power. He brings the balance that prevents order from devolving into nihilism. He is the spark that ignites the fires, transmuting inertia into ecstasy. Southern deities are generally associated with fire. He is the dynamic, primal element of destruction and creation.

He is a god of the frontier, respecting no boundaries or natural laws. He is a spirit that exists within and pushes against the edges of the mundane world. As the third son, he and his children carry within themselves the hidden secret that has become known as the witch blood.

His father sent him to the holy garden to retrieve the Oil of Mercy, which would heal humanity. However, upon arrival, he was denied entry and could not obtain the oil he sought. Instead, he was shown three visions: first, a dry, withered tree; next, a snake entwined around the trunk; and finally, a newborn baby resting in its branches. He realized that the child represented the Oil of Mercy, destined to heal humanity's sorrows.

After receiving three seeds from the Tree

of Life, he returned with them and placed them in his deceased father's mouth. From these seeds, three trees grew: a cypress, a cedar, and a pine. The first for renewal, the second for purification, and the third for the fecundity of the earth. These mighty trees were eventually felled and transformed into the three wands he would use to work his miracles.

To sign his Black Book is to accept both the challenge and promise of this Holy Covenant. He stands in the doorway to welcome you through. To go through is to accept your role as an outsider. The embrace of his love is the confirmation of the witch's placement outside the village. His is a hyper version of the social compact understood by only a few.

The Dark Lord is known to us as the horned one, Old Nick, Old Scratch, Old Horny, and the Man in Black.

Bless thee, Bottom! Bless thee!
Thou art translated.
— Quince

The Sabbath

n the heart of the forest, where the trees twist skyward like ancient sentinels keeping watch over secrets long buried, the night comes alive with whispers. Brother witches heed the call to gather at midnight. Moonlight trickles through the dense canopy, casting shadows upon the ground as the gathering emerges from the underbrush. Cloaked in dark garments that seem to dance with the flicker of candlelight, the witches arrive, drawn together by an ancient calling—by a promise of unity with the untamed spirit of the Earth.

This is no ordinary night; it is the night of the witches' Sabbath, a clandestine ritual that flickers through the ages like the flames of the bonfire crackling at the center of their circle. These men, marked by their unbreakable bond to the natural world, know their purpose: to celebrate the dark, embrace the forces of nature, and commune with the spirits that bind them together.

As the moon reaches its zenith, casting a silver glow upon the earth, the air thickens with anticipation and they disrobe. The Magister stands as the personifcation of the horned one. His brothers line up and kiss his arse. They come together in solidarity and brotherhood. Their nakedness is a bond of trust.

The witches then form a circle, their hands clasped tightly, a web of energy pulsing between them. They begin to chant, their voices harmonizing with the distant call of night creatures. The melody resonates with the rhythm of the forest—an age-old hymn echoing through the trees, invoking the presence of the elder spirits of the forest.

In the center of the circle lies an altar

adorned with offerings—a scattering of herbs, flowers, wine, and bread. The Magister steps forward, masked in green, leather leaves of his foliate vestment reflecting the untamed nature of the forest. With a graceful sweep of his arm, he ignites the bonfire embers, and flames dance upward, reaching toward the sky.

As the fire blazes, visions of the past coalesce in the smoke—flickering images of those long gone, guardians of the land intertwined with the living. They call upon the elements—earth, air, fire, and water—to witness their gathering, to bless their rituals, and to safeguard their secrets. Each brother takes his turn stepping into the firelight, sharing their stories of love and loss. They raise their voices in song, weaving a tapestry of history, resilience, and binding magic that spans generations.

Underneath the boughs of ancient oaks, the night grows thick with their enchantment. Nature pulses with life around them, and the air shimmers with the power of the earthly. As they dance, their movements become a symphony, an expression of both joy and sorrow—a tribute to the trials they face in a world that denies their truths, a rebellion born from centuries of oppression.

Among the flickering shadows stands a young witch whose heart beats fiercely with conviction. Drawn into the depths of the ritual, he surrenders himself to the moment, the power of the ancestors surges through his veins. He raises his arms to the sky, surrendering his wildest dreams to the moon, hoping to bind them to the very fabric of their reality. In that moment, he understands that the witches' Sabbath is not just a gathering; it is a renaissance of spirit, a reclamation of identity, an affirmation of the queer and untamed.

As dawn breaks and the cock crows, the first light of morning kisses the earth, dispersing the darkness and dissolving the enchantment that has held the night in thrall. The witches begin to extinguish the flickering flames. Still, the energy lingers, woven into the very ground they stand upon—an enduring testament to their gathering, their power, and their freedom in the face of darkness.

In the realm otherworldly, the legacy of the witches' Sabbath continues, echoing through time. It reminds us that we are not just a vestige of history but a living force—the heartbeat of the Earth, resilient & ever-persistent.

The infernal kiss is but the beginning of the conclave. Our love is steeled in flesh and united by the shared bonds of our practice.

Buggery is a communal pact at the heart of the Sabbath

The Red Meal

usk was transitioning into full night, and the moon began bathing the trees in soft grey-blue silver. A young man led his friend into the woods behind his grandparents' house. When the friend asked a question, a gentle finger to the lips silenced him. They stepped beneath the tree line, and the youth briefly grabbed his friend's hand to guide him along the narrowing path in the fading light. He released it quickly, but the warmth lingered between them, sparking independent thoughts.

As they moved deeper into the woods, weaving through spruce boughs and the occasional underbrush, they emerged into a small grassy clearing. At the center stood a tall, ancient oak silhouetted against the dark row of trees at the clearing's edge. Its roots sprawled out, sometimes jutting above the ground like knobby fingers, both holding the earth and anchoring the tree. Closer to the oak, the ground sloped downward, where two roots cradled a small pool of water, its edge rimmed with brilliant green moss. The rising moon cast a silver sheen over the surface, hinting at a hidden spring below. The lower part of the clearing likely squished and sank into blackberry brambles before the woods resumed.

Earlier, the youth had left some offerings beneath the tree: a bowl, a bottle of wine, and a dark loaf of bread. An improvised torch was jammed into the ground a few feet from the tree's base. A few weeks prior, he had stumbled upon a pagan podcast, and its ideas had begun to burrow into his thoughts, growing deeper with each passing day. Though rationality urged skepticism, something unexplainable tugged at him, a vague sense of need fluttering like shadows at the periphery of his mind.

They crossed the clearing, where the friend knelt on the high side of the tree while the youth pressed on. For a moment, all memory of the podcast vanished, and a strange presence unfolded just behind his eyes. It was neither distinct nor tangible but guided him softly, as if a gentle hand had laid upon his back.

He took the bowl and scooped spring water into it, walking in a clockwise circle around the tree, sprinkling water on the ground as he did. In his mind, he called upon the Horned Hunter of the woods to bless their grove, imagining he was unraveling the material world with each step. Returning the remaining water to the spring, he placed the bowl back beside the other offerings.

The atmosphere seemed to shift as darkness thickened, tricking their eyes into perceiving phantom lights dancing in the clearing. The moonlight outlined the contours of the friend's face, highlighting his striking features. He had removed his shirt and tossed it aside, and soon the youth followed suit.

As he settled beside his friend, he picked up the round loaf. Tearing it in half, he revealed it as dark bread. Taking the pieces, he placed them into the bowl and briefly hovered his hand over them. He then lifted the bottle of wine, pouring some into a blue earthen cup that he had brought along. Silently, he offered it to the spirits of the forest.

He passed the cup to his friend, who lifted it to his lips, the scent of it slightly stinging his nostrils. The liquid enveloped his tongue in depth and richness before he returned the cup. In turn, the youth drank, savoring the flavor before pouring the remnants into the bowl and soaking the bread in the wine.

Turning to his friend, he admired the way moonlight traced across his shoulders, leaning in to share a kiss. Their lips parted, and tongues met, an unexpected reverence blossoming between them in this intimate moment. Their bodies pressed close, arms encircling each other tighter, the sensation of bones fusing without pain lost in the embrace. Their auras mingled under the moon, dancing and blending.

That small grove felt alive. The youth imagined a tribe of satyrs lurking at the edge of the woods, their expressions mischievous and filled with secrets.

A sound caught their attention. They looked up together to find a buck had entered the clearing just enough to be outlined in the moonlight against the black tree line. He seemed to tilt his rack toward them, then he hooved the grassy earth, turned, and disappeared back into the woods.

As he disappeared into the darkness, the youth were surprised that the interruption had not broken the magic of their unexpected visitor.

I cannot think you
are akin to man
that you were made of dust
and earth-like things
because the memory
of you always brings
old dreams that aged
before the world began

— Ruth Moore

The Elder Gods

In many mythologies, the current deities ascended after displacing a previous assembly of divine personages. Zeus and the Olympians rose to power by destroying the Titans. The Aesir, the gods of Asgard, displaced the Vanir after a hard-fought war, eventually integrating some of their number, namely Freyja, Freyr, and Njord.

Snorri Sturluson, a 13th-century Icelandic historian, poet, and politician, played a significant role in documenting Norse mythology, including the stories of the Vanir gods. In his works, such as the Prose Edda and Heimskringla, Snorri provided detailed accounts of the Vanir, their characteristics, and their interactions with the Æsir gods. His writings are some of the only sources contributing to our understanding of Norse and related mythologies today.

Alaric Hall, an expert on Medieval English Literature, suggests that Snorri's use of the word Vanir was a mistake, perhaps a mistranslation or error in transcribing fractured oral tales. Hall posits that the Elder Gods were actually ælf (plural ælfe), an Anglo-Saxon word that would become elves in modern English.

In Old Norse, we find "alfr" (plural "alfar"), and in Old Icelandic, "huldufólk," meaning "hidden people," which has been regarded as synonymous with Icelandic "álfar" (elves). Although these and Anglo-Saxon "ælf/ælfe" undoubtedly share similar Proto-Germanic roots, the respective lore has evolved along different paths over the centuries. One can deepen their understanding through the study of the folklore from each area; however, it is also essential to remember that they are distinct. This discussion is specifically inspired by the concept of mythical creatures known as ælfe held by pre-Christian Anglo-Saxons.

Hall notes that all surviving early references to Old English ælfe are exclusively male. This is telling. It would seem that only with the medievalization and Christianization of the British Isles, did they split into two genders. With the ascendency of medieval Christianity, female elves also arose. At the same time, the nature of these supernatural beings became more sinister.

From this period, elves come down to us in early medical texts where they were blamed for both ills and illness. In medieval medical texts, elves are often mentioned in the context of causing illnesses. For example, Bald's Leechbook includes charms and remedies to ward off ailments believed to be inflicted by elves. These references suggest that elves were thought to cause various physical and mental health issues, such as diseases of the head and mental illness.

In contrast during the pre-Christian era,

ælfwine, meaning elf friend, was a common Old English honorific attesting to their positive perception. Numerous Anglo-saxon names also speak to the high place in which the ælfe were held: Ælf-red, the origin of our modern Alfred, meaning elf-counsel; Ælf-noth or elf-brave; and Ælf-thryth or Ælf-ric both meaning elf-powerful.

While the references from the earlier period may be all male, the words used to describe them are more feminine. They are not handsome but beautiful, for example. They were males possessed of what contemporaries would normally categorize as feminine beauty. These male beings were often described as paired with armed female warriors, known as hægtessan. These violent women and ælfe represent an inversion of gender norms. Elves and weapon-bearing hags were intrinsically queer from the start.

Norse magic is known as seiðr (pronounced SAY-thur). Practitioners, völvas (female) or seiðmenn (male), would enter trance states to interact with the spirit world, perform divination, bless or curse individuals, heal the sick, and even control the weather. Seiðr was considered primarily women's domain. Male practitioners were often described in derogatory ways that characterized them as sexually transgressive.

The term ergi in Old Norse refers to unmanliness, effeminacy, and one who takes the passive role in anal sex. It was used as an insult to describe men who did not conform to traditional masculine roles. In the context of Norse society, practicing seiðr was often associated with ergi, as it was considered an unmanly activity. This perception was deeply ingrained in Norse culture, and men who practiced seiðr risked being accused of being argr (unmanly) and could face severe social consequences, including being outlawed or even killed.

In Late Iron Age Norse culture, men who exhibited passive homosexuality, unmanly conduct, and perceived sexual feminity were considered outside the societal fabric. Men who practiced magic, seiðr, were very much among them.

It seems that the people of the Viking Age had a view of a sexually transgressive type that looks very much like our contemporary homosexual identity. The rise of Christianity and its focus on individual acts of sin de-coupled individual sexual acts from the notion of a definable identity. This discursive shift surrounding acts such as sodomy meant what one did was not necessarily seen as what one was.

By the early American colonial period, buggering someone behind the church was just a singular act of sin that could be purged through confession. It is likely not a coincidence witchcraft and witches became an increasing concern. It may be that the object of concern shifted, but only slightly.

The Old English cognate for seiðr is -siden. Interestingly, Hall notes, in all instances known, the word is used as a suffix almost always paired with ælfe as in ælfsiden. It would seem that the magic being referred to is always Elven magic, sorcery used or taught by the ælfe. -Siden then was the exclusive domain of an all-male, queer race of spiritual entities.

In the witch trial confessions of the 17th century, magical powers are often described as deriving from elves or fairies. Take, for example, Elspeth Reoch, also known as Elspeth of Orkney, an alleged Scottish witch who was tried and executed early in the century. At her trial in Kirkwall on March 12, 1616, she confessed to practicing witchcraft and deceiving islanders by pretending to be mute. Reoch claimed to have received her magical powers from a fairy when she was twelve. She stated that while staying with her aunt in Lochaber, she was given instructions on acquiring these abilities, which included clairvoyance and the power to induce or cure illnesses through chants and using the melefour herb. Of course, her interrogators interpreted her meeting as converse with the Devil or his demons. Reoch was found guilty and sentenced to death by strangulation and her body burned.

* *
*

(53)

As the lore evolved with society, the Old English ælfe became Middle English elves and then became fairies. By the Victorian era, the magically queer beings had become diminutive, fickle fairies, such as Iolanthe and Tinkerbell. Of course, by the late 19th and early 20th centuries, the term fairy also became slang for gay men. It was initially used to describe men who exhibited effeminate behavior or dressed flamboyantly. Over time, it became a derogatory term used to mock or belittle gay men for perceived unmanliness, reflecting societal prejudices and negative stereotypes.

The ælfe have suffered the generation loss of a copy of a copy of a copy. They are not gone, just forgotten. Their lore is not lost. It lies dormant in the natural worlds, waiting to be re-revealed. Just as we have transformed the slang term and made it our own, we can reclaim our spiritual heritage embodied in these queer elder gods.

In Geoffrey Chaucer's Canterbury Tales, written in the Late Middle Ages, the Wife of Bath laments the loss of fairies and elves, seeing them as replaced by Christian friars and other holy men. But even in Shakespeare's time, it would seem that some of the ælfe's queerness remained. It is hard to eradicate such deeply engrained myths.

At the end of the play, Puck sweeps.

All too often, we find ourselves overwhelmed by anxiety. We may experience personal anxiety with or without an identifiable cause. In a nation where mass casualty events occur far too frequently— such as the increasing number of school shootings and incidents like the truck attack on New Year's Day in New Orleans— we observe national anxiety. At times, we may become engulfed in a whirlwind of global apprehension, confronting political instability as country after country slips into near despotism, the rise of right-wing backlash, environmental catastrophes, and species extinction.

In this modern age of insecurity, spirits, including the present-day ælfe, are accessible to us. As we cultivate our relationship with them, they stand beside us. They are among us as we traverse our path, they march with us when we gather for pride. They are present at the edge of our reality. They linger in the shadows of the bar and are there in the dark corners of backrooms.

I'll follow you. I'll lead you about a round,
Through a bog, through bush,
through brake, through brier.
Sometime a horse I'll be,
sometime a hound,
A hog, a headless bear,
sometime a fire,
And neigh, and bark,
and grunt, and roar, and burn,
Like horse, hound, hog,
bear, fire, at every turn.

– Puck

The (K)Ing of the Ælfe

ut of the enigmatic richness of Anglo-Saxon mythology, Ing emerges as a powerful figure, often intertwined with the Norse deity Freyr, also known by the name Ing Freyr. Both the Norse and Anglo-Saxon deities embody the essence of fertility, prosperity, and the eternal cycle of life, but Ing, in particular, holds an important connection to the world of the ælfe, serving as their revered king. Evidence suggests that with Woden and Thunor, Ing Freyr was one of the most preeminent among the Anglo-Saxon pantheon.

Ing is a wise and benevolent ruler, radiating peace and abundance. We can see this in the norse kenning, Fégjafa or God of Wealth or Abundance. His continence evokes verdant green fields, blooming flowers, and sunlit groves. Again, one of his kennings is Árguð God of fertility or more aptly the "fertile season." The air about him is thick with the fragrance of nature's bounty. Clad in garments woven from the finest threads, adorned with intricate patterns that reflect the beauty of the natural world. Instead of a sword, his weapon is an antler. His hair is golden as ripe wheat and flows like silk. His eyes gleam with the knowledge of the ancient earth and its hidden mysteries.

As King of the Ælfe, Ing is not just a deity of agriculture but a guardian of harmony between the realms of the seen and the unseen. Like the otter, he traverses the two worlds. He presides over the woodland glades where the ælfe dance under the moonlight, their laughter mingling with the rustling leaves. Ing is our bridge between mankind and these ethereal beings, encouraging unity with nature and reverence for its cycles. He guides lost travelers through the darkened forests, revealing pathways where flora and fauna thrive. His spirit nurtures both the land and its inhabitants.

Ing, or Freyr, is one of the Elder Gods, Snorri's Vanir, and, as noted above, likely surviving in the ælfe. He is particularly revered for his connection to agricultural fertility, which made him a significant deity for farmers and those dependent on the land. Freyr is known for his association with the sun and rain, vital for good harvests. Some stories recount how his wooden effigy, shaped like a giant cock, was paraded through the villages.

In Norse mythology, one of his most famous attributes is his magical ship, Skidbladnir. This ship could always find a favorable wind and was large enough to hold all the gods and their equipment. His companion, a boar with golden bristles, named Gullinbursti, symbolizes wealth and prosperity and was created for him by the dweorh or dwarves, likely another name for dark ælfe.

Ing is associated with an unusual weapon: an antler. Rather than a traditional sword or spear, he wields a magical antler that signifies his deep connection to nature and the fertile earth. This weapon, sometimes described as a magical stag's antler, embodies the life-giving forces of the natural world.

According to Norse myths, Freyr's famed sword, which could fight independently, was given away as part of his courtship of the giantess Gerd. Left without his sword, Freyr uses an antler as a makeshift weapon during the final battle of Ragnarok. The antler represents his connection to resourcefulness, even in adversity.

The antler symbolizes Freyr's dominion over vegetation and harvest, representing abundance and fertility. It can summon nature's forces in battle, entangling enemies with flora or invoking wild creatures. This connection reflects ancient Scandinavian respect for animals and links antlers to male vitality and the cycles of nature. Freyr's weapon signifies that true power comes from harmony with nature, highlighting that strength lies in physical force and nurturing the world.

His antler embodies the balance between conflict and harmony, representing a deity of both war and fertility. The Elders offered prayers and sacrifices to ensure bountiful harvests, seeking his favor and protection. Like the sound of bubbling brooks, his laughter was said to bring good fortune, and his blessings invited the growth of bountiful crops and harmonious communities. The tales of Ing remind us of the inescapable relationship between humanity and the natural world—a bond drafted in respect, gratitude, and the eternal dance of life.

In the ancient lore, Ælfheim, or Ælfhame/Ælfhame, the enchanting realm of the ælfe, was bestowed upon Ing Freyr as a revered toothgift, a potent symbol of affection and allegiance among the gods. This gesture, laden with significance, marked a pivotal moment in the cosmic tapestry where realms intertwined. Ælfheim is depicted as a land of ethereal beauty, where luminous glades are adorned with flowering meadows, crystalline streams, and grand sylvan canopies, all bathed in a perpetual golden light that reflects Freyr's essence as a deity of fertility and abundance. The light ælfe, elusive and enchanting beings, dwell within this magical domain, their laughter echoing through the trees and their dances casting a spell of harmony upon the land.

Freyr's acceptance of Ælfheim not only affirmed his dominion over this divine territory but also underscored the profound connection between the natural world and the mystical forces that reside within it, as he embraced his role as a benevolent ruler, fostering prosperity and unity between mortals and the ælfe or fae. This toothgift, emblematic of trust and kinship, further solidified Freyr's status among the gods, establishing him as the bridge between the earthly realm and the mysteries that thrive beyond the mortal gaze. Surrounded by his court, his royal spirit breathes life into the mythic landscape where our lives and their magic intertwine.

Historically, cross-dressing priests have been associated with Freyr's worship in Norse practice. These priests, known in

Old Norse as Freygoði, are believed to have engaged in rituals characterized by the donning of feminine attire, a practice that underscores the fluidity of gender roles in ancient Norse spirituality.

This tradition is further corroborated by the writings of medieval historians, such as Saxo Grammaticus, who documented various aspects of Norse religious practices. According to his account, the Freygoði participated in ceremonial activities that required the adoption of feminine identities, which served as a conduit for invoking the favor of Freyr. These rituals often encompassed sacrifices and other ceremonial acts designed to secure fertility and prosperity for their communities.

By adopting feminine garb and roles, the Freygoði may have not only honored the duality of nature but also reinforced the cultural significance of fertility as a sacred and communal pursuit. The blending of gender in these ceremonial contexts reflects a nuanced understanding of spirituality, where the invocation of divine blessings transcended conventional gender boundaries, highlighting the rich complexity of Norse cultural and religious practices.

Of note, in recent years, much unconfirmed personal gnosis has pointed to Ing Freyr being a god of gay and bisexual men. It may be that his power is not just transgression but also transcendence of normative gender associations. In the Lokesenna, Freyr is portrayed as the epitome of benevolence among the gods, celebrated for his ability to bring happiness and peace, often described as "the best of all the gods of the divine court." The verse highlights that he causes no maid to weep and is no wife to man, underscoring his freedom from normative relationships and, perhaps, a blurring of the binary—though the latter is certainly not unique among the Norse gods. The phrase "from bonds looses all" suggests a liberating and freeing of societal influence.

This portrayal carries significant implications regarding Freyr's ambivalence toward gender and sexuality. On the one hand, his deviation from traditional marital ties (he married a giantess) and his non-possessive nature towards women indicate a fluidity in his identity and relationships that challenges the rigid gender roles of the time. Freyr's character does not conform to the archetype of a god defined solely by masculine authority or dominance but instead embodies empathy and nurturing, qualities that have traditionally been associated with femininity.

Moreover, Freyr's relationships and interactions with both gods and mortals suggest a more complex understanding of desire and attraction that transcends the binary. This ambivalence highlights a multifaceted approach to sexuality in which love and attraction are not strictly defined by societal norms. In this light, Freyr may be seen as a figure who embraces a spectrum of identities and relationships, as well as the interplay between love, liberation, and expectation.

The rune that bears his name is a balanced

symbol. For me, it evokes a specific scene from Kenneth Anger's film Invocation of My Demon Brother. In this brief sequence, two nude young men sit cross-legged, facing each other with their legs entwined. The unicursal hexagram is juxtaposed over them. This could just as easily have been the Ing rune, as its form corresponds well to the magical idiom of the two bodies on screen.

We are familiar with Oberon, the fairy king from Shakespeare's A Midsummer Night's Dream. However, Oberon has roots in medieval literature. It is widely believed to be derived from the French "Auberon" or "Alberon," which in turn comes from the Old German name "Alberich," meaning "elf ruler" or "king of the elves."

Oberon first appears prominently in the 13th-century French medieval poem "Huon de Bordeaux," where he is depicted as a magical dwarf king. The character gained further fame in William Shakespeare's play where he is portrayed as the majestic and powerful king of the fairies, weaving enchantments and influencing the lives of mortals and fairies alike.

In A Midsummer Night's Dream, Oberon embodies a queerness that transcends traditional boundaries of love and desire, reflecting the fluidity of relationships in the enchanted forest. His affection for the youthful and beautiful boy, often interpreted as a symbol of lust and obsession, catalyzes the chaos that unfolds in the play. Oberon's unrequited love for this youth, combined with his cunning nature, drives him to manipulate the magical dynamics around him, intertwining themes of jealousy, power, and transformation. This complex interplay of emotions highlights Oberon's depth as a character and invites the audience to explore the nuances of love that defy convention, illustrating how desire can weave together realms of enchantment and conflict into a whimsical tale.

At the verge, the hare leaping free,
A swift guide to what's yet to be.
The cunning fox, with his sly charm,
Lead us forth, keep us from harm.
A fierce stoat, in hues that shift,
A regal link to the land's ancient gift.
Dive with the otter, where worlds align,
In dreams and waters, wisdom divine.
In nature's embrace, their truths are told,
Guardians of mysteries, both new and old.

Spirits of Place

he phrase genius loci originates from Roman spiritual practice and refers to a specific place's protective spirit or guardian. The concept implies that every place has a distinct spirit that embodies its character, ambiance, and essence. This spirit was believed to watch over and influence the well-being of the location and those within it. In Old Norse, we find Landvættir and in Old English wiht or Middle English wight as in landwights

Landwights are often viewed as spirits or beings linked to specific geographical areas, especially natural features such as hills, rivers, and forests. They represent the ancient belief that the landscape is alive and populated by various supernatural entities.

These beings are generally perceived as guardians of the land. They play a role in the fertility of the earth and the well-being of the community living near them. Landwights were thought to influence the prosperity of crops, the health of livestock, and the overall harmony of the environment. In some traditions, people would offer gifts or perform rituals to appease these spirits, ensuring good fortune and protection for their homes and farms.

The concept of landwights also reflects a broader understanding of nature's interconnectedness within Anglo-Saxon culture. It emphasizes respect for the land, encouraging individuals to live in harmony with their surroundings rather than exploit them. This interaction showcases a profound reverence for the landscape, which was not just a backdrop for human activity but a vital component of life.

Stories and lore about landwights often illustrate their unpredictable nature. While they can bring blessings, they may also respond negatively to those who disrespect or neglect the natural world. This duality serves as a reminder of the consequences of one's actions in relation to the land.

In two surviving medieval glosses, different types of elves were distinguished based on their habitats and characteristics. In a manuscript held in the University Library in Leiden, the medieval scribe penned a list of elves in the margin. He notes muse elves, mountain elves, wood elves, water elves, field elves, and sea elves. To these, the scribe of a manuscript held by the British Library adds "wyld" or wild elves.

These distinctions reflect the medieval fascination with nature and the belief that different supernatural beings inhabited various natural environments. Here, we see supernatural beings associated with forests and woodlands, linked to mountainous regions, connected to bodies of water such as rivers, lakes, and seas, associated with open fields and meadows, connected to domestic settings, etc. Just about all of the loci known to medieval peoples were covered.

Recognizing that these spirits of the land have not disappeared, we may also acknowledge that some have transitioned due to the loss of their original habitat. Some spirits are intrinsically connected to particular locations, such as wells or tombs, while others are mobile. In the historical literature, we may observe that the type of ælf was defined by where they were domiciled, but this relation was not intrinsic. Just as when we move from the country to the city, we go from rural to urban dwellers, these anchored beings may change from wæteraælfen (water elves) to wuduelfe (wood elves) or feldælfen (field elves). They are resilient beings. Our transgression of the natural landscape, industrial farming, and the rise of urban centers and suburbs means that they, too, have had to adapt to new environments. There can be little doubt that we now may find city elves amidst the concrete. Perhaps some of the wood elves have become park elves with which we can commune in the natural islands of the cityscape. Even in the squared order of the modern planned city, a chaotic wildness remains.

The genius loci have always been with us and will continue to be our companions of the land. Our journey is interlinked with theirs. The crooked path is just as much their road as ours. We may befriend them and have supportive company on our journey. The spirits of the land, the elder gods, the ælfe, when we get to know them, are our allies. They are, as one term for the fae reminds us, our good friends.

Outside the Fence

n Norse mythology, the world of humans is known as Midgard (Old Norse: Miðgarðr). It is surrounded by a great sea and the wilderness of Jotunheim, the realm of giants. The gods built a protective fence around Midgard using the eyebrows of the giant Ymir to keep out the chaotic forces. This fence symbolizes the boundary between the orderly, civilized world of Midgard and the wild, chaotic world outside the wall.

In Old English literature, there is the concept of innangard, the middle space, and utangard, outside the fence. The fenced or enclosed space represents order and civilization. Various contemporary texts echo this division, where the inside of the fence is associated with safety, law, and community, while the outside is associated with danger, lawlessness, and the unknown. It is not too hard to picture the walled hill fort or the fenced farmstead.

It is not that Middle Earth is set apart from the other worlds, but itself is partitioned into safe space and the unknown or mysterious. We feel safe at home, but we retain an instinctual fear of the woods at night. This is echoed in the foreboding we may feel walking down a dark and lonely city street. Our visceral fear of what lurks in the dark is instinctual. It is a vestigial hold-over in our evolution.

One of Uppy's most loved poems is "The Hang Downs" where she describes the dangerous cryptids of the Maine woods. These 19th and 20th-century stories were a way for loggers to pass the time, scare newcomers, and share their experiences in the isolated logging camps. The titular creatures were said to inhabit the deep woods. Tales described them as having long, dangling limbs that allowed them to hang from trees and drop down on unsuspecting passersby. The will-em-alone rolled toadstools into balls to bring dark dreams into your sleep. The Sidehill Gouger was a fearsome creature with different-length legs, which defined his unique way of walking. Of course, there too was the Wendigo walking on "his big flat feet." To these, one may add the Tote Road Shagamaw, half-bear and half-moose, said to walk upright on its back legs before switching to its front legs; the Billdad, resembling a kangaroo-platypus hybrid, believed to inhabit Boundary Pond; and the Agropelter, who would throw branches and limbs at unsuspecting loggers. The fact that she envisions this diverse menagerie in a singular location, Bartlett's Island, speaks to the ever-present mystery of the land. They also demonstrate that this New World could be just as terrifying and unknown as the Old.

Immolation &
Emanation

aw, untempered desire is disruptive. It cuts through both law and habit. It desolves the old so that we may manifest the new. The onus is on us to create our own narrative, to weave our own stories. Queerness is an ahistorical fiction.

The first stories were told around the tribal fire. The ancient circle echo in wood and stone those nights when our ancestors came together and encircled the warming flames. Those stories became legends and then myths.

Two birds sit perched above Elysian Fields—a Pheonix and an Eagle. They are sentinals watching over our journey. One reflects the all-consuming fire of our desire, while the other is the fluid expression of our passion.

Desire is inescapable. It will not allow itself to be put aside. It sets us alight and consumes us. We come out on the other side to be reformed.

All too often, the mundane world comes close to destroying us. Like the Phoenix, this immolation gives us agency to rebuild ourselves as we want.

We are the architects of our survival. Our shared desire is a fecund field.

The white eagle is a powerful totem of transformation and transcendence. Noble and resplendent, its feathers flicker like freshly fallen snow caressed by moonlight. It embodies the essence of spiritual heights, soaring above the mundane world, where the everyday entangles the mind.

A creature of the air, the white eagle is both guardian and guide. It is the bridge between the earthly and our hidden desires. Its eyesight pierces through the veils of illusion. His eyes bear witness to the essence hidden within the chaotic dance of passion. He is desire as sacred catalyst. In rising anticipation, he ignites an alchemical process that transcends and lifts us outside the physical.

The white eagle embodies the embracing invitation of our desire. It is the sacred flame gifted to us by the Phoenix. It is the fuel for our forge and the spark that lights the lamp illuminating the path.

In alchemy, the white eagle signifies the transformation of base metal into spiritual gold. The energy shared between brothers becomes an ethereal elixir. It is the ectoplasmic emanation of the seed secreted within. The churning of our well of cum ignites the spirit. The energy rises upwards along our spine toward the crown, just as the eagle's wings beat against the heavens, rising with each powerful thrust.

Our intentional act is reflected in the bird's flight. Its ascension mirrors the energies soaring along our nerves, rising in our bodies. Our union weaves together the distinct threads into a rich tapestry.

As it soars, the white eagle also teaches us the importance of surrender—to the flame of desire, to the flow of intimate sensation of fraternal merging. It entices us to delve deep into the primal forces that bind us together in flesh.

The hidden secret in the imagery of these two birds is this dance of exploration. They encourage us to be individuals and to become magicians, alchemists, and architects of ourselves. Fusing their energies as they reach for transcendence, aligning their spirits with the vast expanses of the universe.

From the fire of the phoenix and flight of the eagle, we emerge transformed, with our hearts a little more open to the third spirit created by our union. In buggery—our raw desires ignite our journey.

Reader, pass on, nor stop to waste your time,
On sad biography, or bitter rhyme;
What I am, this heavy clay ensures,
And what I was is no affair of yours.

– Epitaph, adapted by Ruth Moore

The Guardian

thick mist blankets the earth, and in the distance stands the barrow mound—an earthen dome that rises from the ground like a forgotten sentinel of time. The air is heavy with secrets, whispering tales of lives long past. It is here that the Guardian of the Barrow keeps watch, both feared and revered.

He is cloaked in shadows, his presence an unyielding silhouette against the backdrop of murmuring trees. The Gardian's dark eye sockets seem to reflect the flicker of revenant souls wandering in the moonlit fog. Old stories say he is as ancient as the stones themselves, bound by an oath to protect the resting place of those who once walked the earth. His voice, when it comes, is a low, gravelly rumble that echoes through the stillness, an ancient chant that reverberates against the very fabric of the night.

The mound pulses with life, a heartbeat hidden beneath layers of earth. It appears to breathe beneath the weight of time, each exhalation carrying the scent of damp soil and rustling leaves. The Gaurdian moves with the grace of a predator, every step deliberate yet silent, a guardian rarely seen, always felt. His watch is eternal.

Those who dare to approach the barrow feel the air thicken as if the atmosphere is charged with an omen. Some claim to hear the whispers of the heroes long laid to rest, their valiant tales lingering like an echo in the twilight. Yet, as they step closer, they sense the chilling presence of the Guardian, his gaze like ice. He stands resolute, an arbiter of the threshold, ensuring the sanctity of the dead remains undisturbed.

Legends speak of those brave souls who have ventured too close—drawn by the allure of treasure or the insatiable thirst for knowledge—but found themselves ensnared by the Warden's watchful stare. They emerged forever changed, haunted by visions of the past, unable to escape the weight of history that lingered in his glacial demeanor.

On the island of Orkney, located off the northern coast of Scotland, the legend of the Hogboon exists. The term "Hogboon" originates from the Old Norse word "haugbui," meaning "mound dweller." In Orkney folklore, Hogboons are believed to be ancestor spirits residing in burial mounds. These spirits are thought to protect the land and the families living on it. In exchange for their protection, families would offer food and drink to the Hogboon. However, if the Hogboon was disrespected or not properly cared for, it could bring misfortune to the family.

One well-known story involves the Hogboon of Helliehow in Sanday. This spirit was believed to assist with farm work if it was treated kindly. When the family stopped showing respect to the Hogboon, they encountered disastrous consequences and ultimately had to relocate.

The spirits mentioned in this story seem to have been viewed as a generally positive force. Although their name was introduced by Norse settlers during the Viking Age, the tradition of land spirits linked to specific prehistoric burial mounds likely goes back even further. Making offerings to these mound spirits has a long-standing history and continues in various forms today. This tradition traces back to a time when the worlds of the living and the dead were not so distinctly separated: both inhabited the same spaces. Furthermore, the story underscores that neglecting to honor one's ancestors could lead to negative consequences.

Barrows are an element of the Old World. In the New, we have tombs and graves. But as dusk falls and the world fades into an inky darkness, the Warden of the Tomb, our cognate, takes his place in the stillness, a guardian forever entwined with the ebb and flow of time. Here, in the heart of forgotten lore, he remains a figure of vigilance—a slow, unyielding reminder that some stories are not ours to tell, and in the depths of silence, the past should find its peace.

The Warden stands between us and the other spirits of the land. To enter their realms, we must first approach him and gain his permission. He is the protector of the unnamed dead. He holds their stories, and their weightless truth is at his heart.

The Revenants

ew supernatural entities have evoked as much fear as the revenant. In medieval lore, these spectral beings are the restless dead who returned to the world of the living. Wide-spread concern over the walking, restless dead reflected deep-seated anxiety about death and the unknown.

The term "revenant" derives from the Old French present participle of revenir" meaning "returning" or "coming back." While interpretations of the undead vary across cultures, revenants in England primarily referred to souls believed to have returned to the physical world due to unresolved issues, unjust deaths, or a desire for retribution. Distinct from the more glamorous, or even comical, portrayals of the undead found in later folklore, revenants were typically depicted as ghostly figures with tangible connections to their previous lives—individuals whose earthly concerns remained unaddressed at their passing.

The Medieval period in England was deeply influenced by religious belief, wherein the afterlife was a prominent theme in daily life and spiritual practices. The prevailing Christian doctrine of the time underscored concepts of salvation, damnation, and the purification of souls in purgatory. Concurrently, folk beliefs thrived alongside these religious notions, leading to a complicated dichotomy between official Church and popular folk perceptions of death and the afterlife.

Fear of revenants was particularly acute in rural communities, where tightly knit populations often harbored suspicions about unexpected deaths. It was widely believed that improper burial, untimely demise, or lives characterized by sin could result in a spirit returning to trouble the living. Such fears were exacerbated by a limited understanding of disease, giving rise to tales of the deceased returning to seek vengeance or address unresolved matters.

Medieval literature and oral tradition varied in their descriptions of revenants. They typically depicted them as having ashen or decayed appearances eerily reminiscent of their former selves. Many narratives illustrated revenants haunting familiar places, while others portrayed them as enigmatic visitors to living relatives, delivering urgent messages or unsettling requests.

Tales of revenants seeking retribution were commonplace. One famous story involves the "Wandering Widow," a cautionary figure whose spirit purportedly returned in search of revenge against those responsible for her husband's murder, causing calamities for her adversaries and ensuring that her grievances received acknowledgment, even posthumously.

Communities established various protective measures in response to the pervasive fear of revenants. Proper funeral practices were deemed essential to ensure that one's loved one would stay put in the grave. Garlic or holy relics were sometimes placed within coffins as a precautionary measure. Other customs involved burying bodies with their heads positioned downwards to prevent them from rising again.

The increasing influence of the Church during the medieval period prompted a more organized approach to addressing revenant phenomena. Clergy encouraged families to pray for the souls of the deceased, particularly those who had died without confession or led morally ambiguous lives. The belief in revenants conveniently served as a mechanism for reinforcing societal rules and ethical standards. Fostering fear of the restless dead thus became a tool employed by the Church to keep their congregations in line and to prevent deviation from established norms.

The dead have always been a part of our lives, and some may linger behind to roam the earth. Not all ghost stories are tall tales. When we explore other realms or navigate our own world, we might encounter a spectral remnant of those who have departed. Therefore, it is important to have some tools on hand to handle these unexpected encounters.

Throughout medieval England, traditional precautions against revenants were common. It's good to have at least one witch bottle buried around your property to ward off potential uninvited guests. Witch marks are commonly found in old houses. These marks were used to protect against malevolence and the wandering dead. Garlic, popularized in modern tales of vampires, was also traditionally employed against the restless deceased. Once a year, it is advisable to saine your home. Open the windows to allow them an easy exit. Smoke the house with a burning bundle of juniper.

I wonder what our ancestors would make of the modern world. I imagine it would be like a modern child trying to figure out what a rotary phone was for. In one poem,

Uppy imagines the ghost of Phebe Bunker (1750-1850) returning to her island. When St. Peter's back is turned, she sneaks out of heaven and returns to the Maine island where her family settled. It is deserted and almost unrecognizable. The cellar hole of her cottage is now almost indistinguishable from the surrounding field. She walks to the local cemetery, where she meets the ghost of her recently deceased seven-great grandson Joel. As they sit and talk, her last living descendent nine generations on, visits his grandfather's plot.

He tells of the ills of his time, of the great wars just passed, and the development of the atomic bomb. He notes it's an election year, "a season of the smear." These are trying times, he laments. "Over the sweet, the too-sweet, the corny sweet,/Over the voices calling cheat and traitor and rotten politics,/I listen for the grave and beautiful voice of my country."

He continues his lamentation:

Out of the archives and the histories

(100)

What forgotten sound, blown on by the
         wind,
Of the truths held to be self-evident?
Who say, now?
Jefferson? Whose word creates a flurry
         on both sides among the
         viewers with alarm?
No, nor Lincoln,
Because we have malice it would seem,
         and the cause of clarity is cold;
And shall I tolerate my neighbors or he
         me
Longer than it takes him to kill me
         because I have to try to stand
         him?

Phebe listens and complains that God
should do something to fix the world that
he created, while she knows he's not going
to lift a finger. Her ghostly voice unheard,
she addresses her descendent and the
generations before, echoing the summary
sentiment of the hobgoblin Puck:

You're all the fools of the world and

(101)

always have been.
You could have fixed things up two
thousand years ago,
There was a nice chance for it then,
and any fools can argue out a
difference.
But no; you had to fight it out.
Century after century, and you've still
got to be prancing around and
fighting.
This one's got something someone else
wants;
That one's got a grudge.
Someone's a different color, or thinks
different.
Doesn't matter,
Just so you get an excuse for blood to
flow.

We've certainly had time and chances to prove old Phebe's ghost wrong, but yet, at each opportunity we have proved what collective fools we be.

(102)

And those things do best please me
That befall prepost'rously.
— Puck

The Black Dog

he appearance of the black dog is a frequently occurring theme in British folklore. It is often associated with stories of hauntings and the supernatural. The black dog's appearance is laden with symbolic significance, and it is often interpreted as an ominous harbinger of death or misfortune.

One of the most well-known examples is found in the legend of the Hound of Dartmoor, a spectral hound said to roam the moors of Devon. Described as a large, menacing creature with glowing eyes, this black dog is rumored to be the restless spirit of a man who was wronged in life. Local lore posits that encountering the Hound is a portent of impending doom or tragedy.

(105)

Similarly, the tale of Black Shuck, a ghostly canine reported in the regions of East Anglia, encapsulates the fearful reverence surrounding black dogs. Eyewitness accounts describe Black Shuck as a large, fearsome beast known to frequent churchyards or ancient ruins. Legends tell that those who meet Black Shuck may face dire consequences, drawing on the belief that this spectral dog serves as a warning from the otherworld.

Moreover, in Yorkshire, the tale of the Gabble Retched Knight recounts the story of a spectral black dog that guides lost travelers. While the dog may initially seem to offer assistance, it is also said to lead them astray, further highlighting the duality of the black dog's nature—both a protector and a bearer of ill fortune.

The recurring theme of the black dog in British folklore has a long history in culture. The legend of Black Shuck dates back at least to 1577, when the creature was said to have appeared at the churches of Bungay and Blythburgh in Suffolk. According to the tale, Black Shuck entered the church in Bungay, causing a thunderstorm and lightning, and killed two people who were kneeling in prayer. It then traveled 12 miles to Blythburgh Church, where it claimed two more victims.

In Scotland, one of the most famous spectral black dogs is the Cù Sìth (pronounced "koo shee"). This supernatural creature is often regarded as an omen of death and is linked to folklore involving fairies. The Cù Sìth is believed to guard hidden treasures or serve as a protective spirit. The legend is especially notable on Tiree, where reports of a colossal black dog with paws as large as a man's hand have emerged. Sightings commonly occur near Kenavara Hill, and the dog's appearance is interpreted as a foreboding sign.

There are black dog hauntings in North America. Visitors to the Hanging Hills, including Hubbard Park and Castle Craig, Connecticut, have reported mysterious sightings of the black canine over the years. This legend dates back to the late 19th century and tells of a spectral black dog that haunts a range of volcanic rock ridges in central Connecticut. According to the legend, seeing the black dog once brings joy, seeing it twice brings sorrow, and seeing it thrice means death.

The black dog embodies the fear and the unknown and reflects shared anxieties surrounding death and the afterlife. In modern parlance, the black dog also serves as a poignant metaphor for the experiences of depression and anxiety, embodying the feelings of heaviness, darkness, and an inescapable presence. Much like the elusive creature in folklore, these mental health struggles can suddenly appear, often uninvited, casting a shadow over one's life.

In Goethe's play, Faust comes across a black poodle while walking outside the city walls. He decides to take the dog back to his study, where it eventually transforms into Mephistopheles, the demon with whom Faust makes his notorious pact. The black poodle serves as a symbol of Mephistopheles and his deceptive nature, initially presenting itself as a harmless creature before uncovering its true, malevolent form.

The black dog often shows up unexpectedly. Just as his appearance is often linked with feelings of foreboding and misfortune, depression can feel like a darkness looming overhead, threatening to envelop one in its gloom. Black dog haunting as a metaphor resonates with the experience of an overwhelming sense of hopelessness. This relentless presence can sap one's energy, rob the world of its innate joy, and create a deadening sense of isolation, just as the spectral hound moves through the moors, leaving a trail of despair behind it.

The duality inherent in the black dog tales mirrors the complex nature of mental health. While the black dog may represent a fearsome threat, the sighting contains an element of acknowledgment and understanding. Many have learned to recognize their own "black dog," allowing them to confront and interpret their own struggles. Just as when one encounters a black hound on the moor, the best course is to look at it head-on rather than ignore it. Recognition can be an important catalyst in finding ways to cope, transforming the dark presence into a sign pointing to the path across the misty moor toward healing.

The metaphor also highlights the stigma that is too often associated with mental health issues. Just as the black dog is shrouded in fear and superstition, discussions around depression and anxiety can be occluded by misunderstanding, ignorance, and denial. Bringing these issues out of the silence is crucial in dismantling the fears that surround them, just as the light of dawn can banish the spectral hound that walks in the night.

The black dog symbolizes not only the challenges of depression and anxiety but also resilience and the journey toward understanding. Through acknowledgment, we can transform the narrative from one of fear to one of empowerment, learning to coexist with the shadows rather than allowing them to dictate our lives. Seeing the adversary is a critical step. In many old grimoires, much concern was focused on learning the summoned entity's name. Knowing a creature's name is to gain power over it.

Walking the spiritual path is not always easy. It may ask a lot of us. It often demands introspection, growth, and the courage to confront one's inner demons or spectral dogs. As noted earlier, the importance of self-care cannot be overstated as we trod the path. Nurturing our body and mind is just as important as focusing on spirit. It is essential to maintain balance and resilience along what may seem, at times, a tumultuous journey.

Just as travelers prepare for a long trek by gathering supplies and tending to their needs, the onus is on us to prioritize our well-being to sustain our progress. Engaging in self-care practices—whether through meditation, physical activity, creative expression, or simply taking time to rest—forms a strong foundation from which to embark on deeper exploration. By acknowledging and honoring our own needs, we enhance our ability to navigate challenges as they arise.

By honoring our own needs, we enhance our ability to navigate challenges and cultivate a more compassionate relationship with ourselves, which allows us to be transformatively kind toward others.

Meditation can be an effective method for managing depression and anxiety. Mindfulness practice can be a powerful tool in reducing stress levels. By cultivating a state of non-focused relaxation, meditation lessens the production of stress hormones, which can contribute to feelings of being overwhelmed.

Research has shown that meditation can also alter brain function, especially in regions associated with mood regulation. By changing the way these areas communicate, meditation can help break the cycle of negative thoughts and feelings that often contribute to feelings of anxiety and depression.

Moreover, regular meditation practice stabilizes and enhances emotional regulation. This can, in turn, improve one's ability to manage emotions and cope with the symptoms of anxiety and depression. Focusing on the present moment without judgment can increase one's awareness of one's thoughts and feelings, leading to healthier processing of these experiences. Again, like the haunting hound, seeing it, acknowledging it, and naming it helps to control its impact.

In our modern world, there are numerous pharmaceutical interventions to aid in stabilizing mental health and combatting issues of anxiety and depression. Modern researchers are beginning to examine what traditional healers have known for centuries: that natural remedies can be effective.

Several scientific studies have examined the effects of lavender on anxiety, and they generally show positive results. A systematic review published in 2023 found that lavender essential oil inhalation significantly reduced anxiety levels. The studies corroborated the long-held traditional understanding that lavender can be a safe and effective anxiolytic intervention.

In contrast, the effectiveness of Xanax (alprazolam), a well-known benzodiazepine commonly prescribed for anxiety disorders, may be exaggerated due to publication bias. A 2023 review published in Psychological Medicine found that only one out of five clinical trials showed a positive outcome for Xanax compared to placebo. This suggests that while Xanax can be effective, its benefits might not be as substantial as previously thought.

Caring for oneself is a fundamental and a necessary foundation for practice and overall well-being. Mental health and happiness can be complex, and supporting them often requires interventions from various perspectives.

It is important to note that nothing above should be considered medical advice or a substitute for professional assistance. That being said, there are moments in life when a heathen healer or pagan priest may be just as helpful as a physician.

thick chain hangs down
across hard chest
metal rings frame nipples
circlet of cool metal
warms around thick cock
the hammer of flesh plunges
into the internal fire
the burning desire
of tightening flesh
hips sound on anvil
skin bone sinew
powerful thighs slam
against a lover's ass
ropy strings of cum
stoking the forge
its coals come alive
two bodies meld into one
the ore of desire transformed
by the blacksmith's art

The Smithy

ayland the Smith, also known as Weland or Völundr, is a legendary figure in Germanic heroic legend, Norse mythology, and traditional folklore. Wayland is often depicted as a master blacksmith endowed with extraordinary abilities, particularly in the forging of weapons and artifacts imbued with magical properties. In England, he is particularly associated with Wayland's Smithy, an ancient burial chamber in Oxfordshire. According to local legend, this site is haunted by an invisible smith who will shoe a horse for a traveler if a coin is left on a stone and the traveler does not watch the work being done.

In the traditional story, Wayland was

enslaved by a king, took revenge by killing the king's sons, and escaped by crafting a winged cloak. The Poetic Edda tells his tale in the poem Völundarkviða. The 10th-century Exeter Book contains the untitled Old English poem now known as Deor, which includes the story of Wayland among its anecdotes.

Wayland faced the torment of exile, a formidable smith yet overwhelmed by his sorrow. Countless griefs accompanied him in that frigid dungeon on the island where King Niðhad had imprisoned him. He was bound by numerous strong cords that could hold such a man of his caliber. But this moment of suffering would fade away.

The story of the smithy underscores his dual identity as both creator and victim. According to the texts, he is captured by a king who seeks to exploit his craftsmanship for personal gain. This captivity ultimately catalyzes Wayland's transformation, as he uses his magical skills to enact retribution against his captor. This story's arc reflects broader themes of oppression and resistance. At its core, the narrative highlights the tension between artistic autonomy and subjugation.

The smith's craftsmanship is akin to the transformative power of art and the timeless intersections of creativity, magic, and technology. It would seem that his forges not only produce physical objects but also serve as a metaphor for a crucible for his emotional and psychological turmoil. The artifacts he creates frequently embody themes of fate and destiny, resonating with the epic motifs common to the cultures within which his tale resonates.

The stories of Wayland are, at their heart, tales of the interplay between artistry, identity, and the human experience. The legacy of the magician-smithy endures as a testament to the multiple meanings of Craft. British versions, in particular, emphasize the cunning and resourcefulness Wayland employs to escape from his bonds while also elevating his status from mere craftsman to a semi-divine figure. He ingeniously crafts his tools and weapons, often using the materials his captor unwittingly provided to orchestrate his clever escape.

The craftsmanship behind Wayland's work simultaneously represents physical artistry and ingenuity in confronting adversity through supernatural means. These elements are particularly highlighted in British tales. He is frequently portrayed as a figure interacting with otherworldly beings and invoking magic in his creations. These stories elevate his status from mere craftsman to a mythological or semi-divine figure, bridging the realms of mortals and gods.

The blacksmith's tale remains relevant, highlighting themes of resistance, creativity, and moral justice. The blacksmith, as muscular, sweaty, powerful, and potent with a craft equal to those of the great magicians, is an enduring image. The portrayal of his strong yet cunning resistance against oppression, the celebration of creative expression as a means of liberation, and the pursuit of justice continue to be available as an archetyp. Even today, the narratives at the center of the lore surrounding the magician-blacksmith can inform contemporary discourse and our magical craft, providing us an option to counter cruelty with creativity, antagonism with craft, and artifice with art.

The Ward Cubes

ard cubes are protective structures or artifacts that safeguard your work from threats. Their design combines mystical and technological elements, making them versatile defense tools.

One of the primary functions of ward cubes is to create a barrier against intruders or hostile entities. When activated, they emit an energy shield that prevents entry or mitigates damage from attacks, providing a haven within which to commune with allies.

In addition to physical protection, ward cubes also serve as a defense against magical or supernatural forces. They are imbued with specific enchantments that repel malicious spells or disrupt the abilities of unanticipated malignant forces that may be attracted to your work. By placing them at strategic points around the circle, you create a stronghold and a fortified perimeter.

To craft the wards, obtain five cubes of wood—one for each element and spirit. Paint each one a color pertaining to its elements: air, yellow; south, fire; west, blue; north, green; and black for the unnamed void at the center.

Consecration of the Ward Cubes

Gather your ward cubes and place them in a circle, with the black cube in the center representing the unnamed void. Light a candle at each cube's position (yellow for air, red for fire, blue for water, green for earth) to enhance the energy. Raise your hands, feeling the elemental energies flow through you, and recite the following:

By air I call thee, swift and free,
Bless these wards to watch over me.

By fire I call, fierce and bright,
Ignite my shield, bring forth the light.
By water I call thee, deep and pure,
Wash away harm, keep my heart secure.

By earth I call thee, fertile and bold,
Root these wards, let their strength
          unfold.

By Spirit I call thee l, guide and weave,
Embrace these wards, let none deceive.
With this circle, I bind them tight,
Guardians of day, protectors of night.
Rampart and protection, surrounding
          me.
As I do will, so mote it be—

Let the candles burn for a while, allowing
the energy of each element to fill the space
before extinguishing them. Your ward cubes
are now consecrated and ready to protect
your journey.

Squaring the Compass

n the time before the arrival of a powerful storm, the wind often seems to come from all directions. My grandmother described this portending wind as "boxing the compass." When we work magic, forces often seem to come to us (or at us) from all points. This is why we cast a circle and ward the quarters. In this act, we create both a boundary and a rampart—a circular mote and a fortress square. It acts as a barrier to keep hostile forces out and a boundary to keep beneficial energies in.

"Squaring the compass" is also a phrase used in modern Freemasonry, symbolizing the pursuit of moral and ethical improvement. In Masonic tradition, the compass represents the virtues of self-control and moral boundaries, while the square signifies integrity and fairness. Together, these tools symbolize the ideal of living a balanced life guided by personal discipline and ethical conduct.

In traditional witchcraft, "squaring the compass" is closely related to creating a sacred ritual space. The compass, often called the Witches' Compass, delineates the ritual area, marking it as separate from mundane space. This practice involves drawing or visualizing circles and other shapes to create a magical boundary where practitioners can perform their workings.

The compass is a space between the worlds where the practitioner can either call otherworldly spirits to him or travel to their domains.

The circle is almost always cast, beginning in the east. The very word "orientation" comes from the Latin word "orient," which means "rising" or "east." Originally, this term referred to the direction of the rising sun and was used to describe the positioning or alignment of structures, particularly churches, with the east. Over time, it evolved to signify the broader concept of aligning oneself or finding one's bearings in various contexts, including the sexual. The actual work conducted within may be re-aligned after the circle is cast as appropriate to the work being done.

First, we cast the circle around, then place the individual wards in their respective quarters and the black cube in the center. Each direction is assigned to one of the elemental forces of nature. We begin with air in the east, fire in the south, water in the west, and earth to the north. In our workings, the elements are also represented by incense, the candle, and the last two in the salty water with which we spurge the circle. The Church transformed these guardians into the four Archangels: Raphael, Michael, Gabriel, and Uriel.

Calling the Guardians of the Quarters

Gather your ward cubes and set at the four cardinal points—yellow for east, red for south, blue for west, green for north. The black cube is placed in the center. It may be placed on or beneath your altar. If you are sitting out at the center of the circle without an altar, You may place the fifth cube between your crossed legs near your cock or just behind your back where your butt meets the ground.

Facing east, say:

> Guardians of the East, I call upon your
>   light,
> Air of intellect, guide me through this
>   night.
> With reason as my compass, wisdom be
>   my sight,
> Ward this space and bring your clarity
>   & insight.

Turn to the south, and say:

> Guardians of the South ignite my inner
>   flame,
> Fire of intuition, ablaze in your name.
> Bring forth disruption, like a wild,
>   dancing game,
> Ward this space with courage & infuse
>   me with the same.

Move on to the west, and say:

> Guardians of the West, like the crash of
>   a wave,
> Water of inspiration, my self you will
>   save.
> My guide from birth to grave,
> Ward this space fresh and brave.

Turn to the northern quarter:

> Guardians of the North, enfold me in
>   your embrace,
> Verdant and fertile, wisdom with grace.

Nurture my growth in this place,
Ward this green and sacred space.
Finally, return to the center of the circle
and the black cube. Say:

Spirit of the void, from which all things
arise,
I welcome your presence, sublime and
wise.
In this circle of power, your silence a
disguise,
Ward this space from prying eyes.

Close with gratitude:

Oh, Wardens of the Quarters, I thank
you today,
For your guidance and presence, come
what may.
With respect and honor, I seal this way,
May your wisdom and light with me
stay.

Ḣallowing the Blade

ron and modern steel have long had a particular utility in various forms of magic. Ⅿetals have always been thought of to hold certain occult properties. Ṫhis is especially true concerning elves, fairies, and other spirits with iron.

Iron has long been regarded as a powerful protective agent against supernatural forces. Ṫhis belief likely arises from iron's inherent qualities of strength and durability, making it a material that embodies resilience. Ⅿany communities in the past have viewed iron as a safeguard against malevolent entities, particularly those associated with the fairy realm.

Among the most enduring symbols associated with iron and occult significance is, of course, the horseshoe. This iconic object was often nailed above doorways as a talisman to repel evil spirits and attract good fortune. The horseshoe's unique crescent shape, combined with its iron composition, was believed to capture and direct positive energies, offering protection to those within the home.

In the past, iron was commonly used to construct fences surrounding cemeteries. These iron barriers served a dual purpose: they protected the living from supernatural disturbances and contained the souls of the deceased. Additionally, placing iron objects in coffins was prevalent, serving as a means of safeguarding both the body and the spirit from restless energies.

In numerous cultures, the term "cold iron" refers to unadulterated iron untouched by human warmth. Many believed this iron could harm elves, fairies, and other mythical beings. Such was the strength of this belief that iron objects were frequently incorporated into protective charms rituals as well as strategically placed within homes to ward off malevolent forces.

The use of iron was wider than practical applications. It found symbolic significance in various religious practices, particularly by incorporating iron in church bells and lightning rods. These items embodied the authority of the Christian church over pagan beliefs and natural occurrences, symbolizing the power to tame and control supernatural elements.

Iron frequently emerged as a potent weapon against magical beings in medieval literature. Tales from that era often portrayed iron as possessing intrinsic defensive properties that could repel or even harm these supernatural creatures, emphasizing its status as a formidable barrier between the human and otherworldly realms.

The witch's blade in this type of work is a defensive tool. It is used to draw the circle when its properties as a rampart are emphasized. The blade may also be employed to ward off or banish unwelcome, uninvited, or unwanted visitors. Performing magic is akin to having the curtains open on a well-lit, warm, and inviting window on a cold night. You may certainly attract the guest(s) you've invited, but you may attract some party crashers as well.

The Ritual

Stand in the center of a secluded and safe space. With the blade in hand, visualize a circle of protective light surrounding you. You will need bowls of spring water and wine, plus at least one lit candle.

You might walk in a clockwise direction to establish a type of circle while saying:

I cast this circle round and true,
a sacred space for work anew.

Hold the witch's blade over the bowl of spring water, saying:

By water, I cleanse this tool,
free from the energy that used to rule.

Sprinkle a little onto the blade.
Next, sprinkle the blade with drops of wine,
saying:

> By this wine, I bless this blade,
> With strength and power,
>   all fears dismayed.

Now masturbate. After climax, anoint the
blade with your semen and say:

> With my seed, I take my stand,
> To hallow this blade in my hand.

> With this seed, I call on power,
> To hallow the blade in this sacred hour.

The closing charm:

> As the moonlight shines
>   and the shadows fade,
> I weave my magic into this blade.

> Banish fear, let courage stay,
> As I wield this blade, come what may.

A circle of strength, a ward of grace,
With each whispered word, we seal this
place.

Bound by the water, earth, and flesh,
By this charm this steel refresh.

In the time before time's first dawn,
From their womb sprang all that is born.
They are the Sun, our radiant star,
And the celestial gems, their crown from afar.
They are the earth, sturdy and bold,
Beneath our feet, and distant sight to behold.
They are the water in the rain's sweet fall,
Calming our thirst whenever we call.
They are the salt of the boundless sea,
Flavoring our tears and setting them free.
They are the fire in the hearth's warm light,
Warming those we cherish day and night.
Their legs are the ancient dolmen's might,
Welcoming as we journey into the last night.

The Hazel Wand

azel trees, known for their slender branches and distinctive nuts, were an important resource for early Britains. They played crucial roles in their daily lives and cultural practices. Hazelwood was valued for its flexibility and durability. It was known to last longer than similarly used willow. During particularly cold winters, willow would become brittle, while hazel could last several nights.

Hazelwood was commonly used to make wattle, an important construction material for building fences and structures when woven with other woods and plastered with clay or mud. Hazel was also utilized for crafting tools, baskets, fishing rods, walking sticks, and wands.

The wood from hazel trees was an essential source of fuel. It burned well and was used for heating and cooking, making it a vital resource for early communities. The tree's nuts were a staple food source, rich in fats, proteins, and vitamins. They provided a significant nutritional boost, especially during the colder months when they could be stored easily and when other food sources were scarce. Archaeologists have found numerous buried hazelnut stashes throughout Britain.

Traditional medicinal herbalists used the bark and leaves of the hazel tree, which were believed to have healing properties. They used these to treat various ailments, such as fevers and inflammations.

Coppicing is an ancient woodland management technique involving the periodic cutting back of trees to ground level to promote new growth. Hazel was particularly suited to this method because it responds well to coppicing, regrowing quickly, and providing a steady supply of wood without the need to fell entire trees.

The management of hazel coppices was often a communal activity involving coordinated efforts to harvest and sustainably maintain these resources. This practice, born from necessity, fostered a sense of community and shared responsibility for natural resources.

Hazel coppices support a rich diversity of wildlife. The practice of coppicing creates a variety of habitats, promoting a flourishing ecosystem. Birds, insects, and small mammals thrive in these environments. Research into how our ancestors tended their environment shows that they coppiced some hazels while trimming others differently to promote nut production.

The hazel tree is deeply woven into the fabric of lore. It symbolizes ancient wisdom, transformation, and a mystical connection to nature.

The hazel rod emerged as a powerful tool in dowsing, an ancient method for locating water and hidden treasures. Esteemed by magic practitioners, these rods were thought to possess special abilities due to the tree's deep connection to the earth. The hazel rod's effectiveness in revealing concealed truths amplifies its status as a symbol of discovery and divination.

Hazelwood was also known for its protective attributes. Crafted into magical wands, amulets, and charms, hazel items were designed to shield individuals from malevolent forces and negative influences. Branches of the hazel tree were often hung above doorways, serving as guardians against evil spirits.

In addition to its wisdom and protective attributes, the hazel tree is intertwined with themes of fertility and love. In many cultures, hazelnuts were presented to newlyweds as symbols of abundance and prosperity, signifying a fruitful union. Rituals surrounding the planting or harvesting of hazelnuts were celebrated to ensure the continuation of family lineage and the promise of new life.

Hazel wands have a long and storied history in folklore and magical practices, particularly concerning ælfe, fairies, and spirits. Many late medieval and Renaissance grimoires contain rituals in which one or more hazel wands are an important component. They are often utilized for protection or as an aid in traveling to the otherworld, the land of Ælfhame.

Hazel wands were believed to have the power to bridge the gap between our world and the realm of the spirits. They were used in rituals and spells to communicate with and summon the ælfe. By using them, the magician tapped into the long-held wisdom and mystical properties associated with the hazel tree.

Hazel wands were often used as protective tools used in encounters with fairies, warding off mischievous or malevolent intentions. They were also thought to help the wielder navigate the complexities of the fairy world, providing guidance and insight.

Hazel wands may be used in divination practices to communicate with spirits and seek their guidance. The wisdom of the hazel tree can detect hidden truths and foresee future events. Hold the wand in your dominant hand and focus on your question. You can use the wand to draw symbols or letters in the air or on a surface. Pay attention to any sensations, thoughts, or images that arise.

Hazel wands were traditionally used to summon and banish spirits and the dead. They were also used to delineate sacred spaces, especially for rituals involving spirits.

The wood for the wand should be cut on a Friday during the period of the waxing moon. Preferably, when the moon is in an air sign—Gemini, Libra, or Aquarius, once you have selected a tree, ask its permission to take a branch before cutting. Before taking your leave of the woods, leave an offering, such as a piece of fruit, at the base of the tree.

Through regular use, you form a personal connection with your wand. As the bond strengthens, the wand becomes an extension of your will.

By the grace of earth and sky,
With every breath, the spirits nigh,
Wand of hazel, both strong and true,
I call upon the morning's ancient dew.

Through the roots and branches high,
With whispered winds, I softly tie,
Woven threads of magic bright,
Guide my hand with sacred light.

Blessed be this wood of old,
With your wisdom, brave and bold.
Bring me clarity, strength, and peace,
As I seek your powers to release.
By the power of the witch's art,
May you serve a sacred part.

Bound in love, and shielded from harm,
With this wand, I make this charm.
As I will, so mote it be,
In harmony with earth and sea.
With this blessing, magic flows,
In heart and hand, the power grows.

(151)

Sitting Out

I n ancient Norse culture, the practice of sitting out, known as "útiseta" in Old Norse, held significant magical and spiritual importance. This tradition involved individuals or small groups venturing into the wilderness, often secluded in remote natural settings such as forests or mountains, for extended periods of meditation, prayer, and spiritual communion. Útiseta was not merely a form of solitary retreat; it was a profound ritual practice aimed at connecting with the divine, seeking wisdom, and harnessing supernatural forces.

Sitting out involves setting aside time and space to commune with nature spirits, gods, and ancestors. It was believed that by withdrawing from everyday life and immersing oneself in the natural world, individuals could gain insights, receive visions, or attain spiritual guidance. This practice requires a disciplined mindset, as participants often fast, meditate, chant incantations, or perform rituals to enhance their spiritual experiences.

Sitting out is also a means of gaining insight and magical prowess, granting practitioners access to the hidden powers of the multiverse. As they engage with unseen forces, they may acquire deeper knowledge of healing herbs, divination techniques, or the secrets of the natural world. The solitude and intensity of the practice can help awaken latent abilities and forge a deeper connection to other realms.

The sagas depict individuals enduring harsh conditions and confronting both inner and outer challenges to prove their dedication and courage. These experiences were approached with profound reverence for the sacred and a willingness to undergo spiritual trials for the betterment of both the individual and their community.

Exercise: Meeting the Man in the Fog

Find a comfortable and quiet space to sit or lie down in a relaxed position either at your altar or outside. Close your eyes gently and begin to take slow, deep breaths. Inhale deeply through your nose, feeling your lungs fill with air, and exhale slowly through your mouth, releasing any tension or stress with each breath.

As you continue to breathe deeply and rhythmically, visualize yourself standing at the edge of a serene forest. A gentle mist envelops you, creating a soft, comforting fog that obscures the details of your surroundings. The air is cool and refreshing against your skin, and you sense a profound stillness all around you.

You're walking slowly and purposefully into the misty forest. Each step brings you deeper into the quiet embrace of the fog. With each breath, feel yourself becoming more relaxed and attuned to the tranquility of the forest.

As you walk deeper into the fog, notice

how the mist begins to clear slightly ahead of you. You sense a presence, a figure standing calmly amidst the swirling fog. As you approach closer, you discern the outline of a man emanating a peaceful and gentle energy.

This man exudes the confidence of one possessed of great wisdom yet also has a sense of warmth and kindness. His eyes reflect a depth of knowledge and compassion, inviting you to approach him with openness and trust. You feel a sense of reverence and curiosity as you stand before him, knowing intuitively that he has wisdom to share with you.

Take a moment to observe this wise man. Notice his attire, demeanor, and expression. Allow yourself to absorb the serenity and wisdom that radiate from him, knowing that you are in the presence of a teacher with insights.

Now, silently ask a question or seek guidance in your mind. It could be a question about a challenge you're facing, a decision you need to make, or simply a desire to understand more about yourself and your path in life.

Listen attentively to the man of wisdom's response. It may come as words spoken aloud, a gesture, a symbol, or simply a feeling of clarity and understanding that washes over you. Trust whatever form the guidance takes and allow it to resonate deeply within you.

Take a moment to thank the wise man for sharing his wisdom with you. Feel a sense of deep connection and gratitude for the insights you have received.

As you prepare to leave, know that the wisdom you have gained will continue to guide and support you on your journey. Slowly walk back through the misty forest, carrying a profound sense of peace, clarity, and inner strength.

When ready, gently bring your awareness back to your physical surroundings. Wiggle your fingers and toes, stretch your body gently, and when you feel ready, open your eyes.

Take a few moments to reflect on your

experience. You may want to journal your insights or sit quietly, allowing the wisdom you received to integrate deeply into your being.

Remember that you can return to this meditation whenever you seek guidance or clarity in your life. Trust in the wisdom that resides within you and the support of the wise man you met in the fog.

Icelandic galdrastafur, magical stave or
sigil, for Freyr, recorded by Jón Árnason
in his masterwork Íslenzkar Þjóðsögur og
Æfintýri (Icelandic Folktales and Legends).

Modern Ing-Freyr Sigil

Activating the Stave

e don't know the precise details of how the ancestors approached magic. For example, much of what we know about Old Norse mythology comes from sources preserved in Iceland. However, this information has its limitations, especially considering that Snorri Sturluson and others were Christian monks. Despite these challenges, their accounts can be a useful aid if we keep in mind the constraints of the source material.

We do know that the Vikings and Anglo-Saxons used bind runes, although their usage may not have been as common as in other Germanic cultures. Bind runes are sigils formed by combining two or more runes into a single symbol. They were used for magical inscriptions, apotropaic symbols (meant to ward off evil), or simply as ornamental designs. Several examples of bind runes have survived, particularly Northumbria and Yorkshire, areas settled by Vikings (Danes and Norse) in the 9th century following Ivar the Boneless's conquest of York (Jorvik) in 866.

Notably, some of these inscriptions can be found on Christian objects, including crosses and even an inscription on the coffin of St. Cuthbert. This is not surprising, as is usually the case Christianization often involves a blend of the old and the new.

Icelanders have a long tradition of crafting and empowering magical staves, known as galdrastafir, through a series of rituals, charms, and symbolic inscriptions. Charging and activation are critical components of the practice.

The work begins with the careful selection of materials, which traditionally included lead, wood, or bone. Today, we can also use paper, wood, metal, and more. Choosing a material often depends on the specific magical intention behind the stave, whether it's protection, prosperity, or healing, as well as the material's magical properties.

For example, the Ing stave can be written on paper, burned, or painted on a piece of wood like pine. An antler would also be fitting, as it is connected to Freyr's weapon in Norse mythology.

After crafting the stave, it undergoes an essential process of consecration and activation, which infuses it with its occult significance. To sanctify the stave, one may use spring water or fumigate it with appropriate herbs. This banishes any negative or inappropriate energies from the object and begins its transformation into a magical one.

The activation or energizing stage is pivotal. Here, we pass some of our power into the object. Breathe on the sigil, allowing the warmth of your breath to carry over a bit of you into the stave or bind rune. You may also rub your hands together and pass the heat generated to your creation.

Next, we charge or empower the sigil with our intent. Now, we imbue it with our desired magical intent. Begin to masturbate or, if you have a partner in the working, commence intercourse. Visualize your intended outcome. Focus on your intent. Ideally, the ritual should be aligned with the lunar phases or planetary positions to enhance potency. The choice of timing and location—such as sacred sites or celestial events—can play a crucial role in amplifying the stave's power.

At the point of orgasm, concentrate on your intent. Project that into the sigil. Your concentration should be singular and entirely focused. In the denouement, anoint the object with your cum. In this way, we invoke some of Ing's numinous qualities into our sigil.

Once empowered, the stave can be used in various ways depending on the nature of the object upon which it is inscribed. You may wear it as an amulet, keeping it close to invoke its energies. Alternatively, it can be placed strategically within your home or working space, allowing its magic to influence your environment. The stave can also be integrated into further rituals, where repeated use enhances its effectiveness.

* *
*

A.O. Spare developed a unique way of crafting sigils. Select a word that represents your intent. Remove all duplicative letters. Transliterate the remaining into runes. From these form a bind rune. Lines may be used for multiple letters until the sigil is as simple as possible. Through this abstraction, we create the embodiment of our purpose. Next, these may be cleansed, activated, and charged as above.

Violet Elixir

n folklore, a violet elixir is often depicted as a mystical potion imbued with the enchanting essence of violet flowers. This captivating liquid is not just a simple concoction: it is believed to harbor a wealth of magical properties that resonate deeply with those seeking to harness its power. Practitioners of fairy magic cherish the violet elixir for its ability to promote tranquility, facilitate healing, and enhance spiritual communication.

In A Midsummer Nights Dream, Puck makes an elixir of violets, or wild pansies, to use as a love potion. The fairy king, Oberon, sets out to meet and trick his queen in the place where nodding violets grow.

When consumed or applied in anointing

rituals, the elixir serves as a key to opening one's senses to the delicate energies that permeate the realm of Ælfhame. To embrace its qualities is to invite the ælfe into your life, seeking their presence, wisdom, and guidance in mundane and mystical affairs. Incorporating violet elixir into rituals offers a beautiful way to honor these ethereal beings while requesting their assistance in our magical endeavors.

To make a variant of the violet elixir, in this case, a nonalcoholic syrup, first, collect pesticide-free violets and remove everything except the purple petals. Then, in a small pot, simmer 1 cup of filtered water, turn off the heat, and steep the violets for 24 hours, covered. Finally, strain the liquid through a fine-mesh sieve, pressing out excess moisture.

Return the violet water to a bain-marie, or double-boiler, add sugar (1 cup for every cup of liquid), and gently warm until dissolved—avoid boiling to preserve the color. Add 1 to 3 drops of lemon juice to achieve a clear purple color, but use sparingly to maintain the hue. The syrup may be stored in the refrigerator for up to six months.

When foraging for violets, use only Common Blue Violets (Viola sororia or Viola sororia albiflora) found in shady areas. They should have a sweet, grape-like fragrance and may have a bit of gold in the center. Ensure they are pesticide-free! Be careful to remove all the green parts, as the calyx can turn the elixir brown and impart a bad taste.

One may also use one of several violet-based cordials. Crème de violette, or liqueur de violette, is a violet-flavored liqueur made from a base of brandy or neutral spirit. These sweet and floral European preparations date back to the early 19th century. Available brands include Rothman & Winter Crème de Violette, an Austrian liqueur made of Alpine violets, and another by the French house Giffard, founded in 1885 by pharmacist Emile Giffard in Angers, Loire Valley. These historic preparations inspired the liqueur known as parfait d'amour, the one the Dutch distillery DeKyper manufactures still incorporates violets.

You can also make your own alcohol-based elixir, usually using white rum or a neutral spirit. To create your own herbal infusion, start by adding two tablespoons of common violet petals to a clean, dry, pint-sized jar. Next, pour in two cups of your preferred 80-100 proof (40-50%) alcohol and seal the jar tightly before shaking it well. Let the flowers steep for four to six weeks in a cool, dark place, shaking the bottle occasionally.

Once the infusion reaches your ideal flavor, strain out the herbs using a fine-mesh strainer lined with cheesecloth or a paper coffee filter. Finally, transfer the liquid into storage bottles, cap them tightly, label them appropriately, and store your infusion in a cabinet. It will maintain the same shelf life as the original alcohol.

I know a bank where the wild thyme blows,
Where oxlips and the nodding violet grows,
Quite over-canopied with luscious woodbine,
With sweet musk-roses and with eglantine:
There sleeps Titania sometime of the night,
Lulled in these flowers with dances
and delight.

— Oberon

Skimmed Water Ointment

he Skimmed Water ritual aids in conjuring elves and fairies. A version of it is contained in the Sloane manuscript 3851, a composite manuscript dating to the late sixteenth-century England. There, it is called "To Have Conference with the Faeries."

First, on the night before a new or full moon, you should thoroughly sweep the hearth and place a cauldron, earthen cup, or bucket of clear water on it before sleeping. If your house lacks a hearth, a windowsill or table in front of a window will suffice. The following morning, a jelly-like film may form on the water's surface, which should be carefully skimmed off with a silver spoon and stored in a silver vessel.

Next, set up a table for three, complete with food and drink, on the night of the new or full moon. After applying the ointment to your eyes, light a fire using sweet-smelling wood and sit in silence until three fairies appear. You'll need to ignore the first two, then engage with the third, asking him whatever you desire. This follows a pattern where fairies generally arrive in threes, and there's a tradition of keeping silent upon their arrival.

Another version of the ritual provides slight variations, allowing it to be performed a day before or after the new or full moon. In this rendition, you're instructed to approach the water bucket before sunrise and use a clean saucer rather than a silver vessel for skimming the surface. You'll also need to face the table while invoking the fairy, stating that only the first to arrive is troublesome, and either the second or third can be chosen.

Once you've selected, you're encouraged

to eat from the table and ask him to set a time for another meeting the following day. You should keep the conversation brief and let him leave when he's ready, ensuring you arrive on time for your meeting. It's implied that a connection will persist beyond the initial encounter, hinting at a familiar spirit relationship.

In this version, there's no requirement to sweep the hearth, but a clean towel should be left by the bucket—hinting that fairies may come to bathe. This detail aligns with folklore, where fairies leave gifts in return for clean water and towels, suggesting a shared cultural background with other traditional stories.

The Threshold

he sun dips low on the horizon, casting long shadows that dance among the elder trees surrounding the barrow. As you approach the mound draped in thick green, a chill creeps through the air. The whispers of the forest seem to hush as if holding its breath in anticipation.

The entrance looms before you, a dark, rough square of the void where stone and earth entwine with the ancient roots seemingly outside of time. Pause and feel the weight of countless souls that have passed across the threshold before you. Somewhere deep within, sense the pulse of the otherworld, calling to you with a song only heard by those who dare approach.

Stepping over the threshold, the dim light leads to a chamber illuminated by an otherworldly glow. The air is thick and heavy, laden with ancient energy. In the center stands the Guardian, a skeletal figure majestic and terrifying. His very presence is a tempest of power. Clad in robes woven from shadows, his eyes shine like embers in the low light.

"Many come seeking passage, but few find the courage to pay the price," he says, his voice echoing off the stone walls as if the chamber itself had come alive. You can feel the gravity of his gaze, a weight pressing upon you.

"What is the price you require?" you ask, your voice barely rising above a whisper.

The Guardian steps closer, the resonance of his form shifting like smoke in the air. "In the realm you seek, all has a cost. It is not gold or silver that I desire, but something far more precious—your memory of this moment."

A shudder runs through you. The thought of erasing this encounter, this very heartbeat of your existence, feels like losing a part of yourself. Yet the mystery of the otherworld pulses around you, anticipation vibrates in your veins. "What will happen if I agree?" you inquire, torn between hesitation and yearning.

"The memory of your fear, your longing, and this transaction will be forever sealed within these walls. But what you gain is knowledge, perspective: the answers you seek on the other side," he replies, his voice thick with an ineffable promise.

You close your eyes and summon your courage. "I accept," you say at last, conviction strengthening your voice. As soon as the words leave your lips, the air shimmers, and a vine of light wraps around your wrist, binding your promise to his. The Guardian raises a hand, and the space around you shifts, landscapes and moments swirling like a whirlpool in green water.

An echo reverberates across the low stretch of the chamber. You feel a deep, resonant eddy—something is opening. "Step forward, seeker," he commands. You have no choice but to obey.

As you cross the threshold woven of verdant twilight, you catch a fleeting glimpse of your memories—laughter, love, loss—all dissolving like mist before the dawn, settling like dew on all around you. The Guardian's voice lingers hanging in the air like a whisper mingling with the wind. You sense he is now your guide through to the unknown.

With a final tepid tinge of uncertainty, you step across the threshold and into the otherworld, ready to embrace whatever awaits you on the other side, bearing the price of your passage while surrendering the moment that brought you here. You know not what awaits, but you are willing to leave a part of yourself behind to uncover it.

(180)

Up and down, up and down,
I will lead them up and down.
I am feared in field and town.
Goblin, lead them up and down.

— Puck

Befriending the Fae

everal of surviving English grimoires have methods of befriending the ælfe, described as the Januvian Fairy or Gnome Ritual. In the esoteric realm of ritual magic, Sloane manuscript 3824 delineates the intricate processes of summoning ethereal beings, alternatively referred to as fairies, elves, or gnomes. During the moon's waxing phase, the magician is instructed to traverse to a sacred space where these enigmatic entities reside. By erecting a protective circle and intoning a lengthy invocation from the witching hour until the early morning, the magician seeks to coax a manifestation of the spirit. If the summoned being offers its camaraderie, the magician is to embrace this bond.

Particularly noteworthy are the parallels drawn between this ritual and other practices, such as the Sylvan Square. In these, the magician is urged to prepare a written demand before conducting the conjuration, ensuring that their intentions are clear. The rituals necessitate a deep understanding of more ceremonial magical conventions as they require the magician to employ binding incantations and dismissals, yet the text does not offer explicit formulas, trusting in the magician's knowledge and skill.

In the Januvian Fairy Ritual, the magician steps into the night after the new moon, setting a table as an offering for the elusive fairies. Here, the invocation resonates with the power of names—"Mycob and Oberion"—summoning one of the seven mystical sisters to respond to the magician's entreaties. The requirement to inscribe the request prior to summoning emphasizes the importance of thoughtful intention in the spiritual dialogue that follows.

The process unfolds over seven nights, with the magician reciting the invocation in a rhythmic chant nine times an hour. There's an exhilarating tension in waiting for the fairy to grace the magician with his presence, holding the promise of mystical knowledge and interaction. If the spirit remains elusive, a more forceful invocation is included to bind the spirit. Cajoling, forcing, and binding a spiritual entity shows the influence of the magical evocation of the grimoire tradition, where the entities sought were often characterized as demons. Forcing one to appear is not the best start to a friendship.

In all, these rituals encapsulate the profound dance between desire and the arcane, where the energies of the many realms converge. The practice offers the magician a chance to forge a connection with the unseen, the unknown, and the ultimately transformative power of Ælfhame.

Oberon's Plate

ne of the earliest extant fairy summoning rituals dates to the late 15th century. It is preserved in the Bibliotheca Medicea Laurenziana in Florence. The illustration of the plate depicts a woodwose or wild man.

The image of the wild man, or woodwose, gained significant popularity from the fourteenth to the sixteenth centuries. It was often depicted as a rugged, hairy figure embodying the primal forces of nature. These mythical beings were seen as guardians of the woods, representing a raw, untamed aspect of humanity that stood in stark contrast to the civility of the courtly world.

Artworks and literature of the time

portrayed the wild man as a symbol of both chaos and freedom. These natural eruptions were often juxtaposed with themes of civilization and social order. The wild man was sometimes depicted wandering the forests, interacting with humans and animals. This enigmatic figure captured the popular imagination of the time and served as a reminder of the wildness that lurked just beyond the boundaries of human society.

In British folklore, the woodwose, often called the "wild man of the woods," remains a captivating figure embodying the untamed spirit of nature. He is typically depicted as a large, hairy, and primal creature found in dense forests or remote wilderness areas of the Isles. The woodwose represents a duality of chaos and freedom, serving as both a guardian of the natural world and a symbol of humanity's underlying wild origins.

As evidenced above, the woodwose's origins can be traced back to medieval and Renaissance traditions, where it was frequently featured in folklore, literature, and artwork. An more ancient antecedent is the Greek Pan and the satyrs.

This figure is often depicted as a sharp contrast to the societal norms of the time, embodying the raw, untamed aspects of nature that stood in opposition to the civility and order of the courtly world. As a folkloric character, the woodwose is typically seen as a benevolent, if somewhat mysterious, protector of the forest, capable of interacting with both human beings and the creatures of the wild. In various tales, the woodwose is portrayed not only as a wild creature but also as a figure of wisdom, possessing an understanding of the natural world that is absent in civilized society. This aspect makes the woodwose a symbol of the importance of maintaining a connection with nature, emphasizing a balance between humanity and the wild.

Additionally, the woodwose has been associated with themes of transformation and rebirth, often appearing in stories that explore the transition between the civilized and the primal. Some legends suggest that encountering a woodwose could lead to enlightenment or a deeper understanding of one's own nature, urging individuals to embrace their instinctual inner wilderness. This enigmatic figure celebrates the untamed, reminding us of the timeless allure of the wild and the unknown.

Cast your circle in a private garden or secret place. Burn a fumigation of elder or thorn tree such as myrrh. Place the plate upon your table and have an offering of violet elixir nearby. Beside these place your blade and hazel wand.

Invocation of Oberon and His Court

Take up your wand and hold it over the image on the plate, saying:

O Oberon, great King of Ælfhame,
Thou who reigns in realms
    of shadow and light,
With thy crown of stars
    and mantle of twilight,

(190)

We call upon thee,
        sovereign of the unseen,
Guide us with thy wisdom,
        majestic and serene.
From the depths of
        the enchanted glades,
Where violets nod and
        the whispering breeze sways,
We gather in reverence,
        our hearts open wide,
Seeking the presence of thy ethereal
        court by our side.
Grant us thy grace
        and ancient lore,
As we honor the magic
        that dwells evermore.
O glorious Oberon,
        with thine eyes like the moon,
Awaken the spirits
        who dance in the bloom.
Let the fragrant violets
        summon their kin,
To join us in this rite,
        where the magic begins.
With the sweet notes of nature

(191)

and the vibrant tide,
We invite the elves to stand
here in pride.
O attend to our plea,
O heir of the wild,
In our rituals,
be ever beguiled.
Bring forth thy charm,
and bless us with ease,
As we honor the essence
of earth, air, and trees.
In this sacred moment,
we pledge our intent,
May the harmony of Ælfhame
be ever present.
By the light of the stars
and the depths of the night,
We summon thee forth
to guide us in flight.
O Oberon, King of the Elves,
hear our call,
We open our hearts,
may your magic enthrall.
In this circle of trust,
let our spirits arise,

(192)

As our words weave
      through the worlds.
So mote it be!

As the elven king manifests, offer up the violet liquid and and thank him for being with you.

Be grateful for his appearance. Sit with him and commune. Converse with him and heed his words.

Once you have completed your work, thank him for the guidance, protection, or inspiration he provided during his stay. This acknowledgment makes the departure a natural conclusion to a shared experience.

Raise your wand again above the plate and give him license to return to his realm. With your heart full of gratitude, say:

Return to your sacred grove.
By earth, stream, and sky go in love.
May peace and joy remain in this space,
As you journey back to your enchanted
      place.

S	A	T	O	R
A	R	E	P	O
T	E	N	E	T
O	P	E	R	A
R	O	T	A	S

The Devil's Square

he Devil's or Sator Square is an enigmatic Latin palindrome arranged in a 5x5 grid, reading the same forwards, backward, and diagonally. Some suggest a translation of: "The sower, Arepo, works (or holds) the wheels with care." The meaning of "Arepo" is unclear, and the phrase's true meaning remains hidden. The earliest known examples of the Square were found in Pompeii, dating back to before 62 CE. Over time, it has been discovered in various European locations across many centuries. It later became associated with early Christian symbolism and the "Our Father" prayer, also known as the Pater Noster.

Since antiquity, the Sator Square has been linked to magical and protective properties. It makes appearances in numerous medieval texts and artifacts. Its enduring presence has only added to its mystery.

The Sator Square was often employed in the old grimoires for its protective properties. It was attributed with the power to ward off evil, protect against harm, and bring good fortune. The square's palindrome nature was considered a powerful talisman, embodying harmony and balance, making it a powerful talisman due to its symmetrical and balanced design.

The Sator Square also appeared in various medical texts, where it was used as a remedy for ailments such as rabies and insanity and as an aid in childbirth.

Examples have even been found far from Rome, including in Northern Europe. A fragment of a wooden bowl bearing a partial inscription of the Sator in runes was discovered in Gotland. Other examples, some inscribed in metal drinking cups, have been found in Gotland, Norway, and Sweden. These artifacts have been dated to

Obtain a wooden bowl. Inside it, inscribe, burn, or paint the square in runes, as shown above. The vessel may now be used by placing slips of paper with written requests into it. The slips may be anointed with oils and burned after a time to send the wishes off.

Interlude

n history, cultures such as Scandinavian and Anglo-Saxon understood there to be two seasons, not the four we identify with today. This interplay between summer and winter was deeply woven into the mythic landscape and daily life of these ancestors. Its influence can be seen in everything from agricultural practices to spiritual beliefs.

Summer, in good growing years at least, was associated with abundance, vitality, and the cycle of growth. For the Anglo-Saxons, this season marked the height of agricultural productivity, when crops were in full bloom and communities gathered for harvest celebrations. The Anglo-Saxon Calendar, with its focus on the tides of the year, highlighted this time with festivals reflecting gratitude to deities such as Ing, the god of fertility and agriculture. Summer was a period of rejoicing, where feasting, storytelling, and communal gatherings were common.

In Scandinavian mythology, summer is frequently depicted as a time when the world is alive with color and activity. The sun goddess, Sól, rides her chariot across the sky, symbolizing warmth and life. This season is portrayed through tales of gods and heroes engaging in their quests under the long, bright days of the Nordic summer. Midsummer was celebrated with bonfires and rituals that honor the sun and ensure the earth's fertility, marking a time of renewal and solar energy. Farmers invoked blessings from the gods for a fruitful harvest, understanding the intrinsic connection between their survival and the cycle of nature.

Conversely, winter held its own significance in both cultures, embodying themes of hardship, survival, and introspection. For the Anglo-Saxons, winter was a harsh and perilous time. It demanded careful planning and preparation. The biting cold and potential for scarcity tested communities. The celebration of Yule, with its feasts and merrymaking, emphasized light's return and the hope of renewal as the days began to lengthen following the solstice.

In Scandinavian folklore, winter is imbued with a mystical quality, often represented by the frost giants and the harsh landscapes where survival is fraught with peril. Norse mythology illustrates the winter fields of Niflheim, where cold and darkness reign. Yet, winter also serves as a time for reflection and storytelling. The long nights fostered gatherings around the hearth, where tales of the gods. Lore tells us that Óðinn ventured into the wintry realms to gain wisdom. In pursuit of the well of Mimir, which is located in the land of the frost giants, Jotunheim. There, he sacrificed one of his eyes to drink from the well, hence the kenning Hoárr or one-eyed.

The arrival of the solstice at Midwinter brought with it hope for the return of light, celebrated with feasts and rituals to ward off the cold and invoke protection from the frost giants.

In her novel Spoonhandle, Uppy writes, "Winter in northern seacoast land is interlude." It is a time to repair and reflect. Maine fishermen would over-haul their gear, build traps, paint buoys, mend netting, and chop more wood for the fire. Winter months are a contemplative, quiet time bookended by the fertile growing season. "Walking through the snowy twilight," Uppy writes, winter "is like walking through a dream, and the house looming in blown whiteness is a house of sleep."

Winter can be a time of introspection, but it can also reinforce loneliness. It is a cold time, Uppy tells us, where "content comes out or loneliness bites deep, depending on whether people are content or lonely." The shortest days of the year are times of spiritual vigilance. The festivals of this time serve as reminders that in the shortest, darkest nights, spring and light will come in their time. Loss is followed by new life.

Farmers and cottage gardeners are acutely aware of the change in seasons. In Maine, the growing season is incredibly short, running from the last full moon of May, if the ground is dry enough to plant, to the first hard frost of late September. Most of us may have lost the occupational or survival necessity of an awareness of the changing of the weather with the seasons, but the tides of the year still exert that pull in almost instictual ancestral memory.

In New England, everyone knows the feeling of walking outside and experiencing the first kiss of spring when the air is warm under a clear sun, a light breeze banishing the crisp bite of winter. The same is true in the fall when the first frost ghosts the morning dew in ice crystals. There is always that one maple that goes red-orange early, portending the coming cold.

Uppy was an avid amateur gardener. For decades, she kept a small notebook noting changes throughout the natural year. Each spring, she recorded the arrival of Sam Peabody, the White-throated Sparrow, whose name is a mnemonic for his distinctive call. She noted the day the crocus appeared, the asparagus poked its spears above the ground, and when volunteer lettuce seeded from the previous season surprised the observer. She would note the first snow in the fall or early winter.

Although the changes in the seasons in southern Louisiana may be attenuated, there is still a difference between the two halves of the year. We rejoice when the first cold front of the fall drops temperatures below eighty degrees Fahrenheit. Though we often buy our Yule tree while wearing shorts and t-shirts, we get one or two hard frosts a season. Likewise, in late winter and very early spring, there occur days that remind me of the first touch of warm air along the Maine coast.

Understanding the seasons enhances our connection to nature and the cyclical patterns of life. Our lives are intertwined with the mythic landscape and the eternal dance of summer and winter. These dualities remind us of the alternating pattern of joy and struggle, abundance and scarcity, that reminds us that this, too, shall pass.

The Field Remedy

ver generations, humanity has inflicted lasting harm upon the environment we inhabit. A pervasive mindset, one that perceives us as separate from or even superior to the natural world, has fostered an insidious indifference towards the planet we share. This sense of disconnection has deepened through the centuries, especially as the relentless pursuit of progress and prosperity accelerated with the dawn of the Industrial Age. The consequences of this voracious appetite for consumption are glaringly evident, and they manifest in the degradation of ecosystems, loss of biodiversity, and the destabilization of climate patterns.

Despite the growing awareness of

environmental degradation, the transition to renewable and sustainable resources has been painfully slow. We continue to encounter significant headwinds, often fueled by a collusion between denial and the seductive allure of the expedient. These challenges are compounded by overbearing economic interests and a lack of political will, hindering meaningful change.

As we navigate our path, we will likely experience a profound shift in our relationship with nature. The once-clear lines that separate us from the natural world, as well as the distinctions between within and without, present and future, begin to blur. With each step towards greater awareness and empathy, we come to realize that we are not merely individuals but rather unique cells in a vast, interconnected organism. Our mother is the sun that nurtures our existence, the earth that provides sustenance, and the water that sustains life. Our father is found in the field and forest, embodying the resilience and interconnectedness of all living beings.

In embracing this perspective, we open ourselves to the understanding that our well-being is intrinsically linked to the health of our environment. By cultivating a sense of stewardship and responsibility, we can begin to heal the wounds we have inflicted upon our planet. It is not too late to redefine our relationship with the natural, to honor it not as a resource to be exploited but as a living entity deserving of respect and care. Through collective action and a commitment to sustainable practices, it is possible to foster a future where harmony between humanity and nature is not just an ideal but a reality.

Witchcraft is not supernatural but max-natural. As walkers along the Crooked Path, our power and that of nature are intrinsically linked. Though we stand between worlds, able to move from one to the other like the otter from land to sea, we know no particular is more important. The existence of all worlds is interdependent. Even the gods and goddesses draw on us to remember them into continued robust existence. Together, we can nurture our planet and ourselves, paving the way for future generations to thrive within this intricate web we call life.

As we seek to understand our inter-relationship with the land, we will likely feel inspired to do our part in healing what we can. Industrialization, world wars, and modernity have left lasting scars on the planet, and it is crucial to recognize that our sacred spaces are not merely areas we set aside and honor; they also require our active efforts to improve. Our ancestors understood that their survival depended on a healthy environment. Early farmers learned to rotate crops and avoid depleting the soil, while livestock was often cross-bred with a neighbor's animals to enhance genetic variation and vigor.

Before we move too far down the path, it is wise to offer healing to the land immediately around us, even if it is just a small patch of soil. In the past, farmers practiced a charm known as the "Field

Remedy" or Æcerbot in Old English. This ritual was used to heal barren fields or those thought to be affected by malevolent forces. It consists of several steps to restore fertility and productivity to the land.

The traditional method involves a series of steps performed at night and the following day. First, before dawn, four sods are taken from each corner of the field, and their positions are noted. Next, oil, honey, yeast, and milk from all livestock on the land are collected. Additionally, pieces from every type of tree (except hardwood) and herb (except burdock, as it is generally considered a nuisance being naturally invasive and hard to control) that grows on the land are gathered.

These ingredients are then blessed with holy water and squeezed three times onto the base of the sods. A prayer is recited, asking for the land to grow and prosper. This prayer includes references to the Christian Trinity and the Lord's Prayer (Pater Noster).

After the blessings, the sods are taken to

a church, where a priest sings four masses over them. Once this is done, the sods are returned to their original positions in the field. Four crosses made from quickbeam wood are then crafted and inscribed with the names of the four evangelists: Matthew, Mark, Luke, and John. Finally, these crosses are placed in the field, and a concluding prayer is recited.

Though the above has Christian overlays, its underlying pagan elements can still be discerned. It is easy enough to repurpose this for modern use. Before dawn, take four small patches of earth from each corner of the field, noting their original positions. Next, gather a blend of organic materials, such as honey, yeast, and milk. Additionally, collect twigs or small branches from every type of tree (excluding hardwood) and a selection of herbs, preferably those you have grown yourself.

These gathered materials are then combined and infused with positive energy. This can be done through a personal meditation or a group gathering where intentions for the land are shared and focused upon. Once this has been done, the materials should be carefully spread over the base of the earth patches while stating your hopes for the land's revival. Once completed, return the earth patches to their original corners in the field.

Next, create four markers from wood (preferably rowan/ash, Old English cwic-beám) or similar natural material and write empowering words or symbols representing growth, abundance, harmony, and renewal. Finally, place these markers in the field and conclude with a moment of reflection or additional positive affirmations, envisioning a flourishing and productive land.

In the Dark

n the dark recesses of the world, shadowy backrooms, or isolated fens, individuals gather, compelled by the primal and fierce desire that grips them. These meetings occur in places that feel deeply connected to the earth itself, a realm influenced by ancient and elemental forces. Within these hidden locales, a mysterious sort of priesthood emerges—one that seems to be intertwined with the dark essence of the underworld, drawing power from its depths.

These individuals, akin to otherworldly beings, partake in an enigmatic ritual that involves consuming a strange, sacred substance, a life-giving elixir. Their behavior defies explanation, as if under the influence of a powerful force that transcends normal understanding. Their actions, wild and untamed, reflect a connection to something primal and timeless, leaving outsiders baffled by the intensity of their gatherings and the inexplicable bond that unites them.

In the witches's eyes, the priests performing these arcane rituals possess throats resembling deep, shadowy tunnels. Their mouths serve as gates to uncharted passages that delve into the primordial depths of existence. At the very heart of this mystical journey into the unspeakably wicked deep lies the old ones, the ancient guardians of the all-powerful wand cloaked in secrets and shadows. Surrounding them, the elder gods stand in their magnificent grandeur, patrons of gold and fire. Their presence is a testament to the divine and the profane. Within this sacred space, fumigated with an incense of sweat and the acrid chemical smell of poppers, lie the keys to enlightenment, waiting to be discovered by those brave enough to seek them.

In an era reminiscent of the time before

history was etched into stone, our temple becomes wherever we are, a fluid sanctuary shaped by our experiences and emotions. We find our kindred spirits in the sultry shadows of New Orleans, gathering upstairs at the Phoenix, the Eagle a place alive with whispers of the past and echoes of the present. Here, we embrace the dark, united as priests of a fraternal order born from the primordial abyss. Ours is an ancient cultus, instinctually drawn together, devoted to worshipping at the fountain of the white elixir that flows from our very souls.

Each ritual we perform, each word we chant, binds us further to the mysteries we seek to unlock. We become conduits of ancient knowledge, channeling the energy of the ancient races as we delve deeper into the entwined realms of the seen and unseen. It is in this nexus of darkness and light that we unearth our true purpose—an awakening to the profound truths hidden within the fabric of existence. We are not merely seekers; we are the torchbearers of eternal wisdom, forging a path into the unfathomable night that awaits us.

(217)

Hail to the Givers, a wanderer appears,
Where shall he find warmth amidst chill and fear?
He seeks the hearth's glow, a refuge fire,
Longing for comfort, as the cold winds conspire.

Numbed to the knee, from the journey he bears,
With hunger and thirst, his soul slightly tears.
He craves food and clothing, a sheltering hand,
Eased from the trials of the rimy-strewn land.

Drink offer, for a thirst yet unquenched,
With kindness extended, and hospitality trenched.
Marks of good fortune, in friendships sincere,
Welcome him in, let joy draw you near.

A traveler must move on his way,
And never in one place too long stay:
For if he rests too long on borrowed ground,
What once was loved may swiftly turn to wrong.

— Inspired by the Hávamál

The Repast

uring the cakes and ale ceremony, we share with the gods. At the red meal, we offer to the spirits of nature and the intelligences of the land. When we eat in silence during the dumb supper or mute dinner, we share with those who have departed. When we share our food and drink with our brothers, we also share our love sitting with them in brotherhood. Coming together in a safe space, offering our abundance freely without expectation of return underscores our mutual bonds of trust.

Neighbor taking care of neighbor was at the heart of the ancient social compact. The act of sharing our abundance with our brothers is an embodiment of our pact.

Our promise is not just with the Dark Lord. When we place our signature in his book, we also pledge ourselves to all those who have signed before and will sign after. The covenant is also one of brotherhood and mutual support. We give freely, knowing that our kindness will be returned to us in our time of need.

When the ancestors gathered around the communal fire to listen to each other's stories, they shared in the bounty of the tribe and wisdom of the elders.

Archeologists have discovered the bones of over 1,000 livestock animals at Durrington Walls, a massive Neolithic settlement and henge enclosure near Stonehenge. The overwhelming majority of the bones are from pigs, with the remaining from cattle. These findings suggest that large-scale feasting events took place in the area, with people and animals traveling from various parts of Britain to participate. The bones show signs of being roasted and cut with flint tools, indicating communal meals and celebrations.

When we come together, we are not just offering up our bounty to the gods; we are also sharing it with each other. Breaking bread and filling our brother's cup is as vital today as it was to the ancient ancestors.

In the Hávamál, an ancient Norse text attributed to Óðinn, offering a guest a drink is crucial. One's hospitality reflects the host's honor. Slaking the newly arrived guest's thirst establishes trust and camaraderie between the host and visitor. It's a gesture that signifies respect, imbues warmth, and strengthens community.

Blōtmōnaþ, or "Blood Month," was the Anglo-Saxon month corresponding roughly to our modern November. This month marked a time when livestock were slaughtered in preparation for the winter months. It was a transitional period, with the harvest feasts having concluded and the hardships of winter approaching.

In every feast we partake in—whether sacred or communal—we invoke an age-old ritual of connection. The act of gathering, sharing, and celebrating life binds us to our past while forging new roads to the future. Through these shared meals, we affirm our commitment to community, spirituality, and the relationships that nourish us. We honor the traces of history that are the roots of our practices. The simplest of acts can echo a profound legacy handed to us through generations.

It is a reminder of the power of togetherness in a world that often pulls us apart. We are never truly alone. When the magister fills the cup with mead, ale, or wine, the gathered brothers partake first, and the magister drinks last. As we pass the cup or drinking horn, we affirm our fraternal equality and the equipoise underlying our pact.

He wanders the wide world, in need of his mind,
For simple is solace when home's paths we find.
Yet the wise may take note of the fool who displays,
In the company of sages, talk in empty ways.

Let not a man boast of his mind's great might,
But watch o'er his wits, lest they take flight.
Cautious and silent, to doors let him tread:
For those who are heedful find little to dread.
No truer companion in life can be found
Than the wealth of wisdom with little sound.

To the wary wanderer seeking a place,
Let silence befriend him, and tune him with grace.
With sharpened ears listen, and eyes open wide:
For wise men discover the paths to stride.

– Inspired by the Hávamál

The Dumb Supper

he Dumb Supper, also known as the Mute Supper, is a traditional ritual with roots in Scotland and the Appalachian region of the United States. It involves preparing and consuming a meal in complete silence, often intended to connect with the spirits of ancestors or seek guidance for the future.

In Scotland, the Dumb Supper was traditionally held in the fall around Halloween, or Samhain, a Gaelic festival marking the end of the harvest season and the beginning of winter. The ritual was believed to honor the dead and invite ancestral spirits to join the meal. Participants would set an extra place at the table for the spirits and eat in silence, hoping to receive messages or signs from their ancestors.

In the Appalachian region, carrying on a Scottish tradition, young women seeking to find their future husbands often practiced the Dumb Supper. The ritual involved preparing a meal in complete silence, setting the table with an empty chair for the prospective spouse, and waiting in silence for a sign. If a man appeared and took a seat, it was believed to be a sign that he would be her future husband. The practice was also thought to bring good luck and protection.

Today, the Dumb Supper has been adopted within Pagan and Wiccan communities to honor ancestors and connect with the realm of the departed. The ritual often includes elements of silence, candlelight, and offerings to those who have gone before.

I often hold a dinner between the final harvest festival, Harvest Home, and Halloween. All attendees are asked to leave their mobile devices in a basket by the door. The electric lights are switched off, and candles light the dining room. We set a place for the ancestors at the table, complete with a life-sized skeleton. We dine in complete silence.

At the end of the meal, we toast the departed. In conclusion, as we would with any guest, we thank them for joining us and wish them safe travels back to their abodes.

As with the repast, when we share our abundance here, we do so with all our brothers, both living and dead. It is a time to remember the vital role played by those who walked the path ahead of us.

In addition to those we know, it is also important to remember those we did not. We lost a generation of gay men to the Holocaust of the AIDS pandemic. We can also welcome these unknown and, to us, unnamed in our remembrance. As the old saying goes, that which is remembered lives.

With our imprint, the Library of Homosexual Congress, my co-curator Tom Cardamone and I have established a tradition of releasing a book written by someone lost to AIDS on World AIDS Day, December 1st. I find this to be some of the most important work we do.

More recently, when excess mortality is taken into account, we lost almost fifteen million people globally to COVID-19. Our grove lost one of our brothers, the Bayou Brujo, early in the pandemic. We remember him during our All Hallow's feast and honor him on his birthday.

I have lost more brothers to suicide and substance abuse than to natural causes. This is not surprising as gay men are four times more likely to attempt suicide in their lifetimes than their heterosexual counterparts. Multiple factors contribute to this disparity, including experiences of homophobia, discrimination, and social stigma. These negative experiences all too often lead to feelings of isolation, depression, and hopelessness, all of which are significant risk factors for suicidal ideation.

In addition, studies have shown that gay men who die by suicide are more likely to have had a diagnosed mental health condition, a history of suicidal thoughts or plans, and a crisis around the time of death. This is only compounded if there are intersections of multiple minority identities, such as race and age.

My ancestral shrine has too many familiar faces lost too soon.

Research shows that LGBTQ+ youth who have at least one positive role model, just one accepting adult, in their lives are 40% less likely to attempt suicide. This support can come from literally anywhere, be it family members, elders, teachers, coaches, or spiritual advisors. Positive role models can provide a crucial sense of belonging, validation, and support. They help LGBTQ+ individuals feel seen, heard, and know that they are valued. Social intolerance and rejection remain widespread. Each time we share a meal, a coffee, or even just an ear with a dash of advice, we are reinforcing equanimity and organically countering the forces that conspire against difference and oppose equity and equality.

In addition to disease, suicide, and addiction, we have lost far too many of our brothers to violence. The Nazis killed thousands of gay men, though the precise number will likely never be known. Of course, hate did not disappear with the fall of the Third Reich. Even today, we continue to lose our own to senseless acts driven by hate. These victims also have a place at our supper where we honor and remember our other named and unnamed dead.

When I was young, Charlie Howard was murdered in nearby Bangor, Maine. Howard was a 23-year-old man who tragically lost his life in a hate crime on July 7, 1984. While walking with his boyfriend, Roy Ogden, Howard was attacked by three teenagers who harassed and assaulted him for being gay. The attackers threw Howard over the State Street Bridge into the Kenduskeag Stream, despite his pleas that he couldn't swim. He drowned while his boyfriend managed to escape and call for help.

At the time, many blamed the victim. Some claimed he incited the incident by flirting with the teenagers. The homosexual panic defense was used during the trial. The perpetrators were charged with manslaughter and tried as juveniles.

At least one of the assailants was friends with people I know who defended the killing as justified. In high school, I often had young men yelling at me as I walked through the halls: "I hope you know how to swim!" The State Street Bridge was thereafter known to many locals as Chuckahomo Bridge.

This tragic event galvanized the Bangor queer community and led to the formation of the Maine Lesbian/Gay Political Alliance, which later became EqualityMaine. Now, a monument stands along the Kenduskeag Stream to honor Howard's memory. Howard's story inspired writer Stephen King, who included a scene in his novel "It" that features a scene eerily similar to Howard's tragic fate.

In the modern world, we have a collective

amnesia. History, at best, is what happened yesterday, not forty years ago, let alone 1,500.

Our ancestors are more than near-forgotten prologue. They flow with us, echoes in time, and the genes of our cells.

We may feel a justified sense of obligation. Cemeteries are filled with the forgotten. How many of our gay elders lie beneath the ground of New York's Hart Island, the city's potter's field?

As Uppy writes, "The rocks will never miss you, nor the sky/The sea will be unchanging, oh, my dear:/Tomorrow by this water, only I/Of all things else shall know you are not here."

When we remember the dead, we honor both them and the ongoing solidarity of brotherhood. Like the birch, new life springs in the aftermath of devestating loss.

Remember, remember!
The fifth of November,
The day of election & plot,
A rising tide of division and strife.
Racism, hatred, and division,
Cut through our nation,
A shadow cutting like a knife.
Voices that once hoped for unity,
Now clash and divide in the night.
Remember the lessons of history,
As we strive for what's just and right.

...not a mouse
Shall disturb this hallowed house.
I am sent with broom before,
To sweep the dust behind the door.

– Puck